Letts

GCSE

Success

Revision Guide

AQA
Geography

Adam Arnell

Contents

The Earth's crust

Tectonic plates

The Earth's crust is broken into huge slabs of rock called **tectonic plates**. There are seven major plates and several smaller ones. Tectonic plates 'float' on the denser mantle rock beneath. There are two types of tectonic plate. Oceanic plates are 5 km to 10 km thick, continental plates are 25 km to 90 km thick. Oceanic plates are made from denser rock than continental plates.

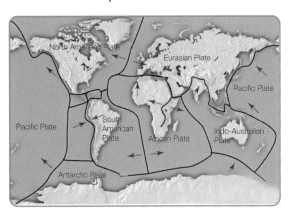

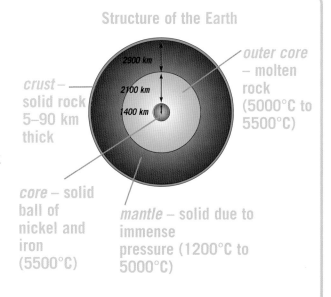

Structure of the Earth

crust – solid rock 5–90 km thick

2900 km

2100 km

1400 km

outer core – molten rock (5000°C to 5500°C)

core – solid ball of nickel and iron (5500°C)

mantle – solid due to immense pressure (1200°C to 5000°C)

Pangaea
200 million years ago all the continents were joined together, forming a mega-island called Pangaea.

Plate movement

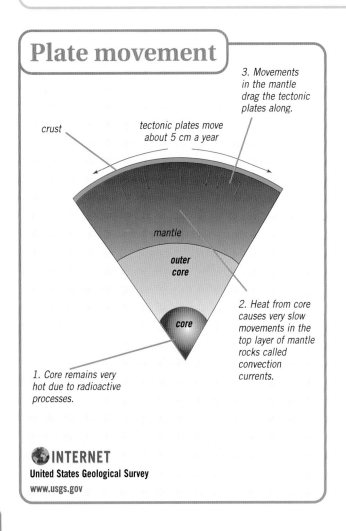

3. Movements in the mantle drag the tectonic plates along.

crust

tectonic plates move about 5 cm a year

mantle

outer core

core

2. Heat from core causes very slow movements in the top layer of mantle rocks called convection currents.

1. Core remains very hot due to radioactive processes.

🌐 **INTERNET**
United States Geological Survey
www.usgs.gov

Fold mountains

Fold mountains are formed where two plates converge. The rocks in the crust are compressed, folded and faulted to form new mountain ranges. Areas of fold mountains include the Alps, Andes, Rockies and Himalayas.

Fold mountains environments are used by people in a number of ways, for example, settlement, tourism, forestry and farming.

Plate boundaries

Plate boundaries, or margins, are the places where two or more tectonic plates meet.

Constructive boundary

- Oceanic or continental plates diverge.
- Mantle rock melts and erupts as lava.
- New crust is formed.
- Undersea volcanoes form mid-ocean ridges.
- Minor earthquakes occur as the plates move.

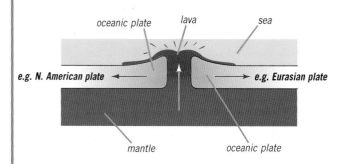

oceanic plate — *lava* — *sea*

e.g. N. American plate ← → *e.g. Eurasian plate*

mantle — *oceanic plate*

Collision boundary

- Continental plates converge.
- Plates are not dense enough to sink into the mantle.
- Plates buckle and form fold mountains.
- There are powerful earthquakes, but no volcanic eruptions.

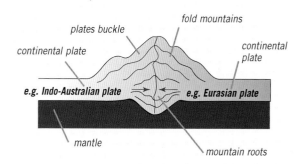

plates buckle — *fold mountains*

continental plate — *continental plate*

e.g. Indo-Australian plate → ← *e.g. Eurasian plate*

mantle — *mountain roots*

Destructive boundary

- Oceanic and continental plates converge.
- Denser oceanic crust is forced down into the mantle (subduction).
- Oceanic crust is melted and destroyed.
- Explosive volcanoes are formed.
- Powerful earthquakes occur as the plates move.

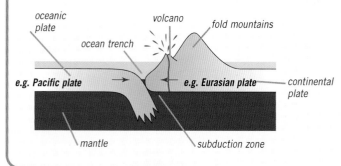

oceanic plate — *volcano* — *fold mountains*

ocean trench

e.g. Pacific plate → *e.g. Eurasian plate* — *continental plate*

mantle — *subduction zone*

Conservative boundary

- Tectonic plates move in different directions, or at different speeds.
- Plates become locked together.
- Pressure builds until rock snaps along a fault.
- Plates move suddenly, causing powerful earthquakes.

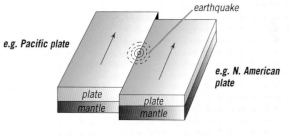

earthquake

e.g. Pacific plate

e.g. N. American plate

plate — *mantle* — *plate* — *mantle*

KEY TERMS

Make sure you understand these terms before moving on!

- collision boundary
- conservative boundary
- constructive boundary
- core
- crust
- destructive boundary
- fold mountains
- mantle
- outer core
- tectonic plates

QUICK TEST

1. What are the two different types of plate?
2. How do tectonic plates move?
3. What happens at a constructive boundary?
4. Where are fold mountains formed?
5. On which plate boundaries are ocean trenches formed?

Earthquakes

Earthquakes are a series of seismic waves (shock waves) caused by movement of the Earth's crust. Approximately 6000 earthquakes occur each year but only a small number cause devastation.

Causes of earthquakes

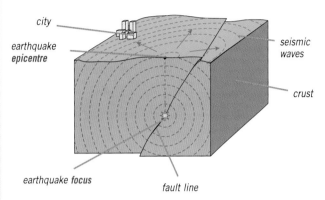

city

earthquake epicentre

seismic waves

crust

earthquake *focus*

fault line

Pressure builds up at plate boundaries

movement is prevented by friction between plates

stored energy is released in a few seconds and travels out as **seismic waves**.

suddenly the **crust** breaks along a fault

ⓘ *Earthquakes may occur many miles from plate boundaries, along fault lines in the crust.*

🌐 **INTERNET**
USGS earthquake information centre
http://wwwneic.cr.usgs.gov/

Case study: Pakistan earthquake – LEDC

Country: Pakistan
Date: 8 October 2005
Epicentre: Muzaffarabad
Strength: Richter Scale 7.6

Cause
Pakistan is on a collision boundary between the Indo-Australian and the Eurasian plates.

Effects
Deaths: 73 000
Homeless: 3 million
Cost: £3 billion (estimate)

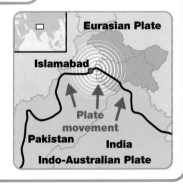

Eurasian Plate

Islamabad

Plate movement

Pakistan

India

Indo-Australian Plate

Case study: Kobe earthquake – MEDC

Country: Japan
Date: 17 January 1995
Epicentre: Awaji Island, Akashi Straights
Strength: Richter Scale 7.2

Cause
Japan is on a destructive boundary between the Philippine Plate and the Eurasian Plate.

Effects
Deaths: 5 000
Homeless: 300 000
Cost: £80 billion (estimate)

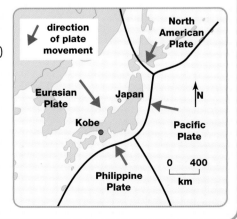

direction of plate movement

North American Plate

Eurasian Plate

Japan

Kobe

Pacific Plate

Philippine Plate

N

0   400
km

Effects of earthquakes

Primary effects are hazards caused immediately the earthquake strikes.
- Buildings collapse, killing and trapping people inside.
- Bridges and elevated roads collapse, crushing cars and people.
- Objects such as signs and glass fall from buildings, injuring people below.

Secondary effects are problems faced after the earthquake.
- Fire breaks out from broken gas pipes.
- Water supply is cut off due to broken water pipes.
- Access is difficult because roads and railways are buckled.
- Disease spreads as there is a lack of food and clean water.
- Tsunami sea waves of up to 30 m may occur in coastal areas.

Long-term effects are problems that may continue for years after the earthquake.
- Unemployment where offices and factories were destroyed.
- Homelessness while waiting for homes to be rebuilt.
- Economic damage as the government spends billions on rebuilding.
- Psychological and emotional damage to those involved.

The Mercalli scale measures the strength of an earthquake by assessing the amount of damage it has caused. The scale ranges from one to 12.

Prediction and preparation

Despite much research it is not yet possible to predict earthquakes accurately. However, it is possible to prepare for them.

- Earthquake-resistant buildings are built with deep foundations made from special rubber. Concrete is reinforced with steel, allowing buildings to twist and sway.
- Emergency plans are drawn up, and supplies such as medicine, tinned food, drinking water, tents and blankets are stockpiled.
- Earthquake drills are held to practise what to do in the event of an earthquake.

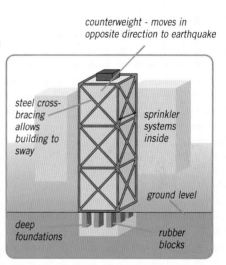

counterweight - moves in opposite direction to earthquake

steel cross-bracing allows building to sway

sprinkler systems inside

ground level

deep foundations

rubber blocks

KEY TERMS

Make sure you understand these terms before moving on!
- crust
- epicentre
- focus
- seismic waves

QUICK TEST

1. What is the difference between a focus and an epicentre?
2. What instrument is used to measure earthquakes?
3. What does the Mercalli Scale measure?
4. Why do LEDCs suffer more damage than MEDCs in an earthquake?
5. Is fire a primary or secondary effect of an earthquake?

Volcanoes

■ A volcano is a cone-shaped mountain formed from lava and ash ejected through a gap in the Earth's crust.

Types of Volcano

There are two main types of **volcano**.

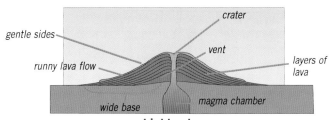

shield volcano

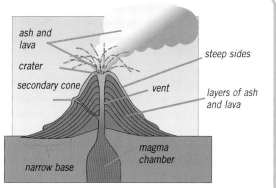

composite volcano

■ Constructive plate boundaries ➡ magma rises to fill the gap as two plates pull apart ➡ relatively gentle eruptions, e.g. Iceland.

Volcanoes are classified as active if they have erupted recently, dormant if they have erupted in the last 2000 years and extinct if they have not erupted for many thousands of years.

■ Destructive plate boundaries ➡ oceanic crust is melted as it is subducted ➡ magma forces its way upwards through the continental crust to erupt as explosive volcanoes, e.g. Mount St Helens, USA.

Prediction and preparation

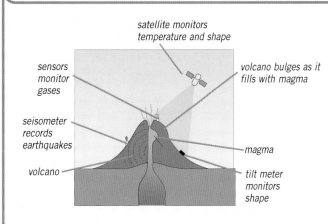

Being able to predict volcanic eruptions makes it easier to prepare for them.
■ Hazard maps are drawn up to show the areas at risk.
■ People are evacuated to safe areas.
■ Lava flows may be diverted by spraying them with water, or even bombing them.

 INTERNET
Volcano world
http://volcano.und.nodak.edu

Benefits of living on tectonic plate boundaries

■ Fertile soils – from weathered volcanic ash and lava.
■ Geothermal energy – steam provides electricity and central heating.
■ Tourism – visitors come to see features such as geysers and bubbling mud pools.
■ Minerals – gold and diamonds are found in volcanic areas.

 Molton rock is called magma when it is underground; lava once it reaches the surface

Montserrat: Case study

Country: Montserrat, Caribbean
Date: eruptions between 1995 and 1997
Location: Soufriere Hills volcano

Cause
- Montserrat is on a destructive boundary between the South American Plate and the Caribbean Plate. Soufriere Hills is a composite volcano.

Short-term impacts
- Pyroclastic flows burned buildings and trees.
- Ash buried over two-thirds of the island.
- Population evacuated to north of the island.

Medium-term impacts
- 60% of housing was destroyed.

- Lack of clean water and sewage facilities.
- No hospital and few schools remain open.

Long-term impacts
- 8000 people left Montserrat as refugees – only 4000 remain.
- Farming impossible as fields are buried under ash.
- Coral reefs are dying under ash washed into the sea.

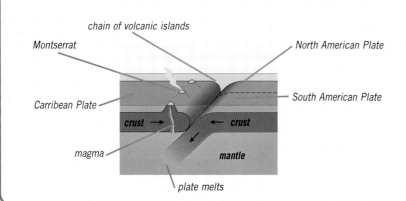

Effects of a volcanic eruption

- **Pyroclastic flow** – cloud of red-hot gas and ash blasts down the side of a volcano at over 200 km/hour.
- **Mudflow** – mixture of ash with rain or melted glacier forms deadly river of mud.
- **Lava flow** – river of molten rock between 800°C and 1200°C.

- **Ash fall** – millions of tons of ash bury buildings, roads and crops.
- Global climate – ash is carried high into the atmosphere ⇨ reflects sunlight ⇨ can make world climate cooler.
- The effects of volcanic eruptions tend to be more severe in LEDCs compared to MEDCs.

KEY TERMS

Make sure you understand these terms before moving on!
- ash fall
- composite volcano
- lava flow
- mudflow
- pyroclastic flow
- shield volcano
- volcano

QUICK TEST

1. What is a dormant volcano?
2. Which two types of plate boundaries have volcanoes?
3. What is a composite volcano?
4. How can satellites help to predict volcanic eruptions?
5. Give two benefits of living on a plate boundary.

Rocks

There are three different groups of rock – igneous, sedimentary and metamorphic.

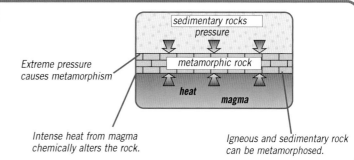

- Hardness – strength of rock – resistance to weathering and erosion.
- Fold – buckled or bent layers of rock caused by tectonic movements.
- Pervious – rock that allows water to pass through joints and bedding planes.
- Permeability – ability of water to pass through rocks.

Rocks and their characteristics

- Joints – vertical cracks in rock.
- Bedding planes – horizontal cracks between layers in sedimentary rock.
- Porous – rock that allows water to pass through pores.
- Fault – fractures running through rocks caused by tectonic movements.

Metamorphic rocks

Metamorphic rocks are formed from sedimentary and igneous rocks during volcanic activity, or earth movements.
- Marble – formed from chalk and limestone.
- Slate – formed from clay and mudstone.
- Quartzite – formed from sandstone.

Extreme pressure causes metamorphism

sedimentary rocks
pressure
metamorphic rock
heat
magma

Intense heat from magma chemically alters the rock.

Igneous and sedimentary rock can be metamorphosed.

Sedimentary rocks

Sedimentary rocks are formed from small particles.
- Chalk – shells of tiny sea creatures; also contains flint.
- Limestone – coral, shells and skeletons of sea creatures.
- Sandstone – grains of sand cemented together; sometimes formed in deserts.
- Clay – particles of silt carried out to sea by rivers.

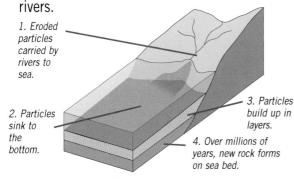

1. Eroded particles carried by rivers to sea.

2. Particles sink to the bottom.

3. Particles build up in layers.

4. Over millions of years, new rock forms on sea bed.

Igneous rocks

Igneous rocks are formed from molten rock – magma.
- Basalt – extrusive igneous rock, dark colour with fine texture.
- Granite – intrusive igneous rock, multi-coloured with coarse texture.

extrusive igneous rocks are formed from lava which cools at the surface

intrusive igneous rocks are formed from magma which cools underground

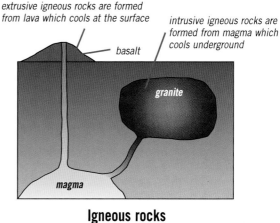

basalt

granite

magma

Igneous rocks

Weathering

Weathering is the natural process of rocks being broken down at the Earth's surface.

Physical weathering – **freeze–thaw**

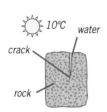 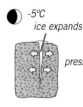 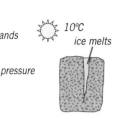

1. Water seeps into cracks during the day.

2. At night the water freezes and turns to ice. Ice expands by 9% exerting pressure on the rock.

3. The next day the ice has made the crack larger. The ice melts and the process begins again.

Chemical weathering – carbonation

1. Rainwater absorbs CO_2 from the atmosphere.

2. Acid rain dissolves calcium carbonate in limestone.

This makes natural 'acid rain'.

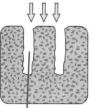

Joints are weak points and are attacked first.

3. Rock joints are enlarged as rock is weathered.

Biological weathering – vegetation. Tree and plant roots penetrate and enlarge cracks in the bedrock. Decaying vegetation releases humic acid which can increase chemical weathering.

Chalk and Clay

Case study

Chalk and clay are sedimentary rocks, which occur together, for example, in eastern and southern England. Chalk forms gently rolling hills called downs, while clay forms wide, flat areas of land known as vales. This landscape is a result of alternating bands of chalk and clay, which have been tilted by tectonic movements. Clay is less resistant than chalk and has been weathered and eroded, exposing the chalk as hills. Chalk hills are known as an escarpment. Steep-sided dry river valleys can be found on the scarp slope. These were formed during the Ice Age when large rivers flowed over the frozen ground.

Chalk and clay landscapes are well populated. Many settlements are found at the foot of the downs, where water comes to the surface as springs. Water stored in the porous chalk is an important source of water for the water companies. Chalk offers good pasture for sheep and, sometimes, racehorses. On the clay vales, animals are grazed and crops grown. Clay pits provide the raw materials for bricks.

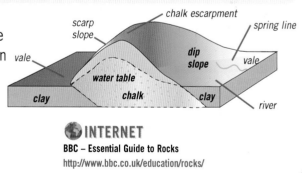

INTERNET
BBC – Essential Guide to Rocks
http://www.bbc.co.uk/education/rocks/

KEY TERMS

Make sure you understand these terms before moving on!
- freeze–thaw
- igneous
- metamorphic
- sedimentary
- weathering

QUICK TEST

1. Which group of rocks is formed from magma?
2. What is chalk made from?
3. Why does freeze–thaw weathering not happen often in very cold areas?
4. What is a scarp slope?
5. What word describes a rock that allows water to pass through its joints?

Landscapes

Carboniferous Limestone

Case study

The Yorkshire Dales is an area of **carboniferous limestone**. Carboniferous limestone is a very hard sedimentary rock, forming upland areas with steep slopes. Limestone landscapes are known as karst scenery. These unique landscapes are a result of limestone's mineral content and structure.

Limestone is made of calcium carbonate, which is slowly dissolved by naturally acidic rainwater. Its surface is weathered along its joints to form a limestone pavement. The enlarged joints are called grikes, and the remaining blocks are called clints. Surface drainage is rare, and rivers disappear down dissolved joints called swallow holes. Underground, joints and bedding planes are enlarged by the flowing water to form pot holes, caves and caverns. In places, the dissolved calcium carbonate is re-deposited to form **stalactites**, **stalagmites** and columns.

When a cave collapses, a depression called a shake hole results at the surface. At Gordale, in the Yorkshire Dales, a large cavern has collapsed to form a steep-sided gorge.

Limestone quarrying in the Yorkshire Dales

Limestone areas are relatively sparsely populated, but do provide a number of opportunities for people. The impressive landscape attracts tourists, particularly walkers. Farming is limited to mainly cattle and sheep grazing. Limestone is a commercially valuable rock, and in places it is quarried to provide material for building, cement, fertiliser and steel making.

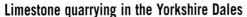

Diagram labels: shake hole, swallow hole, limestone pavement, joint, river, bedding plane, pot hole, gorge, stalactites, cave, stalagmites, river reappears (resurgence)

Arguments in favour:
- quarrying provides jobs for local people
- limestone resources are needed to supply industries with raw materials
- quarries are screened by embankments so are hidden from view
- landscaping after closure will restore the environment.

Case study

Swinden Limestone Quarry, Grassington, Yorkshire Dales
- Swinden limestone quarry has been in operation since 1775.
- The depth of the quarry is 80 metres.
- The quarry will be 120 metres deep by the time it is planned to close in 2020.
- When the quarry closes it will be restored to form a nature reserve with a large lake.

Arguments against:
- the Yorkshire Dales is a National Park
- dust and noise from excavating equipment
- danger from a large number of heavy lorries transporting rock
- water table and water quality may be affected.

Granite

Case study

Dartmoor is a **granite** area in South-West England. Because it is a resistant rock it has formed an upland area. Dartmoor is the result of a major igneous intrusion known as a **batholith** (magma which cooled inside the Earth's crust). Many thousands of years of weathering have exposed the granite. Because it is a resistant rock it has formed an area of high relief. In places, rocky outcrops called **tors** have formed. Chemical and physical weathering have worn away the joints to leave behind blocks of granite. Tors can be between five and 10 metres high.

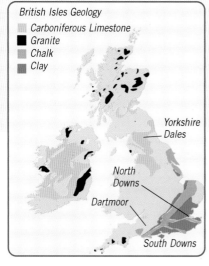

joints enlarged by weathering
granite blocks
rock fragments (scree)

granite batholith   Dartmoor
sedimentary rock

British Isles Geology
- Carboniferous Limestone
- Granite
- Chalk
- Clay

Yorkshire Dales
North Downs
Dartmoor
South Downs

🌐 **INTERNET**
Yorkshire Dales National Park Authority
http://www.yorkshiredales.org.uk/
Dartmoor National Park Authority
http://www.dartmoor-npa.gov.uk

Granite is an impermeable rock, so Dartmoor has many rivers, such as the River Dart. The rivers have eroded steep sided V-shaped valleys. There are many marshes and bogs in places where the water is unable to drain away.

Granite areas are sparsely populated. The soils are too thin, acidic and infertile to grow crops. On the lower slopes sheep and cattle may be grazed. Granite has an important use as building stone. When granite is weathered it forms china clay (Kaolin). China clay is used in making pottery, paper and paint. Dartmoor also attracts tourists. Up to 8 million people pass through every year.

 Practice identifying different landscapes using Ordnance Survey maps.

KEY TERMS

Make sure you understand these terms before moving on!
- batholith
- carboniferous limestone
- granite
- stalactites
- stalagmites
- tors

QUICK TEST

1. What is a batholith?
2. What features formed by weathering are found in granite areas?
3. How are granite areas used by people?
4. How are limestone pavements formed?
5. What is the difference between a stalactite and stalagmite?

River processes

Rivers form an important part of the hydrological cycle. As rivers flow from high land to the sea, they erode, transport and eventually deposit material.

Hydrological cycle

The **hydrological cycle** is the continuous circling of water between the sea, atmosphere and land. Precipitation falling on land finds its way back to the sea following a number of different routes in a river basin system.

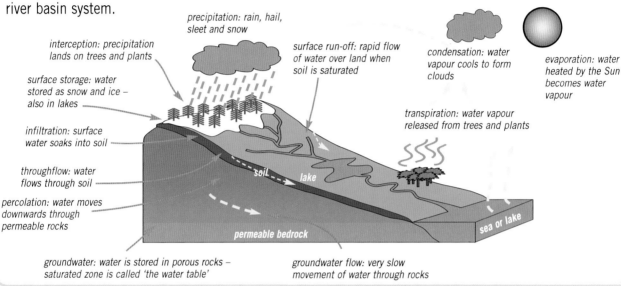

precipitation: rain, hail, sleet and snow

interception: precipitation lands on trees and plants

surface run-off: rapid flow of water over land when soil is saturated

condensation: water vapour cools to form clouds

evaporation: water heated by the Sun becomes water vapour

surface storage: water stored as snow and ice – also in lakes

transpiration: water vapour released from trees and plants

infiltration: surface water soaks into soil

throughflow: water flows through soil

percolation: water moves downwards through permeable rocks

soil   lake

permeable bedrock

sea or lake

groundwater: water is stored in porous rocks – saturated zone is called 'the water table'

groundwater flow: very slow movement of water through rocks

Erosion

Rivers **erode** the land in four ways.
- Hydraulic power – sheer force of the flowing water on the bed and banks.
- Corrasion/abrasion – stones and pebbles carried by the river wear away the river channel (sandpaper effect).
- Corrosion – river water dissolves calcium carbonate in chalk and limestone.
- Attrition – stones and pebbles carried by the river smash into each other, breaking them into smaller pieces and making them rounder.

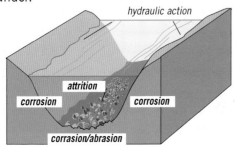

hydraulic action

attrition

corrosion   corrosion

corrasion/abrasion

Transportation

The material carried by a river is called its load. The load is **transported** along the river's course in four ways:
- Traction – rocks and boulders are rolled along the river bed by the force of the water.
- Saltation – stones and pebbles bounce along the river bed as they hit each other and the river channel.
- Suspension – fine particles of silt in the water – river looks cloudy.
- Solution – minerals dissolved in the river water.

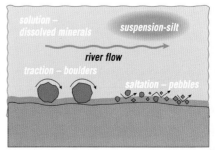

solution – dissolved minerals   suspension-silt

river flow

traction – boulders   saltation – pebbles

Deposition

When a river slows down it loses energy and **deposits** its load.

- A river loses energy when discharge falls, or when it reaches the sea.
- The heaviest material (rocks) are deposited first and the lightest (silt) last.
- The minerals in solution become salt in the sea.

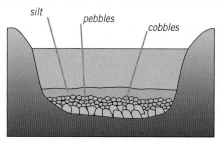

heaviest material deposited first

River valley long profile

- The **long profile** of a river is a cross-section from its source to its mouth.
- Long profiles may be divided into upper, middle and lower course stages.
- River gradients decrease gradually downstream – steep in upper course, very gentle in lower course.
- Long profiles are usually concave in shape – but different rock types make them irregular.

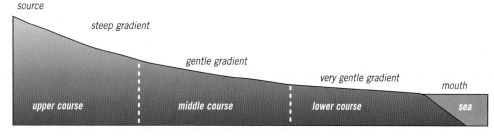

River valley cross-sections

- The shape of a river valley changes along its course from source to mouth.
- Erosion is the key process in the upper course, deposition in the lower course.

Upper course
- narrow V-shaped valley
- steep valley sides
- river erodes vertically
- bedload: angular boulders and cobbles

Middle course
- wider valley
- gentle valley sides
- river erodes vertically and laterally
- bedload: smoother pebbles

Lower course
- very wide valley
- flat valley floor
- river erodes laterally and deposits bedload
- bedload: smooth sand, silt and clay

Discharge is the amount of water in the river. It increases from source to mouth. This is because tributaries add more water to the main channel. As discharge increases, the width and depth of the river must also increase.

Velocity increases from source to mouth. As the discharge of the river increases, there is less friction from the river bed and banks. This means the water is able to flow faster, even though the gradient becomes more gentle.

KEY TERMS

Make sure you understand these terms before moving on!

- deposition
- discharge
- erosion
- hydrological cycle
- long profile
- transportation
- velocity

QUICK TEST

1. What is the hydrological cycle?
2. What causes interception?
3. When does surface run-off occur?
4. Name the four processes of erosion carried out by rivers.
5. Why does river velocity increase downstream?

River landforms

Waterfalls and gorges

Case study – High Force, River Tees, UK

A **waterfall** is a place on a river where water flows vertically. They occur in the upper course of a river.

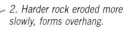

3. Overhang eventually collapses and the waterfall moves upstream.

*4. Steep sided valley called a **gorge** is formed.*

5. Large pieces of rock – remains of previous overhang.

2. Harder rock eroded more slowly, forms overhang.

6. Deep plunge pool is eroded at base of waterfall.

gorge

river flow

waterfall

harder rock

softer rock

1. Less resistant rock eroded more quickly, undercutting harder rock.

Ox-bow lakes

Case study – False River, Louisiana, USA

An **Ox-bow lake** is a horseshoe-shaped lake lying next to a river. They occur in the middle and lower river course.

■ erosion
■ deposition
↘ fastest flow

1

During a flood, narrow neck of land is eroded.

Meander loop becomes very large and inefficient.

meandering

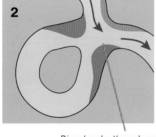

2

River breaks through and follows the shortest course.

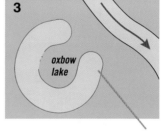

3

oxbow lake

Over time the lake becomes a marsh, and then dries up completely.

Meander is cut off to form an ox-bow lake.

Deltas

Case study – Nile Delta, Egypt

A delta is an area of low lying land at the mouth of a river.

Deltas only form under certain conditions.

■ The river must be transporting a large amount of sediment.
■ The sea must have a small tidal range and weak currents.
■ The sea must be shallow at the river mouth.

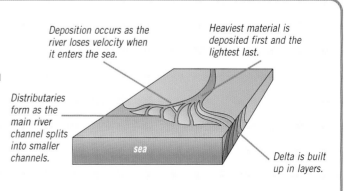

Deposition occurs as the river loses velocity when it enters the sea.

Heaviest material is deposited first and the lightest last.

Distributaries form as the main river channel splits into smaller channels.

sea

Delta is built up in layers.

Meanders

- A **meander** is a curve, or loop in a river.
- Meanders may begin where a river flows round an obstacle.
- Meanders occur all along a river course.

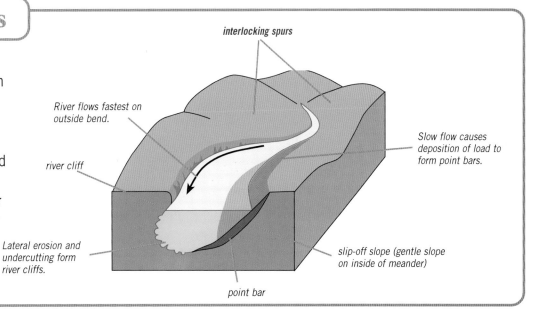

interlocking spurs

River flows fastest on outside bend.

river cliff

Lateral erosion and undercutting form river cliffs.

Slow flow causes deposition of load to form point bars.

slip-off slope (gentle slope on inside of meander)

point bar

Flood plains and levées

- A **flood plain** is an area of flat land formed on either side of a river.
- **Levées** are raised banks of sediment along the sides of a river.
- Flood plains and levées occur in the lower river course.

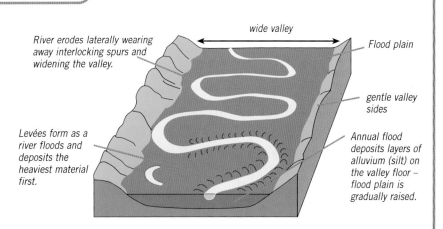

River erodes laterally wearing away interlocking spurs and widening the valley.

wide valley

Flood plain

gentle valley sides

Levées form as a river floods and deposits the heaviest material first.

Annual flood deposits layers of alluvium (silt) on the valley floor – flood plain is gradually raised.

Watershed – the area of high land dividing two drainage basins.

KEY TERMS

Make sure you understand these terms before moving on!
- delta
- flood plains
- interlocking spurs
- levées
- meanders
- ox-bow lakes
- waterfalls and gorges

QUICK TEST

1. Name a waterfall you have studied.
2. What feature is formed as a waterfall retreats upstream?
3. What feature is formed on the inside of a meander?
4. At what point along a river course is lateral erosion dominant?
5. What is a levée?

Flooding

A river floods when the *discharge* is too large for the channel to hold – it 'bursts its banks'.

Causes of flooding

- **Precipitation** – heavy rainfall over a few days ➡ saturates soil ➡ surface run-off.
- Storm – hot dry area ➡ ground baked hard by sun ➡ intense burst of heavy rainfall ➡ water cannot infiltrate ➡ very rapid run-off ➡ flash flood.
- Snowmelt – temperatures rise ➡ snow melts ➡ stored precipitation is released.
- Deforestation – fewer trees ➡ reduced interception and transpiration ➡ increased surface run-off.
- Urbanisation – concrete, tarmac and drains laid ➡ surface becomes impermeable ➡ rapid increase in surface run-off.

Case study : Mozambique floods – LEDC

Country: Mozambique, Africa
Date: February 2000

Causes
- Tropical cyclones brought low pressure, wind and rain.
- Long period of heavy rain (1100 mm over four weeks).
- Very large drainage basin bringing floodwater from Zambia and Zimbabwe.
- Dams overflowed, releasing large volumes of water.

Effects
- 400 people dead.
- 1 million people made homeless.
- Roads, railways and bridges washed away.
- Malnutrition widespread due to lack of food.
- Mosquitoes bred in stagnant water, increasing malaria.

 INTERNET
Environment Agency
http://www.environment-agency.gov.uk

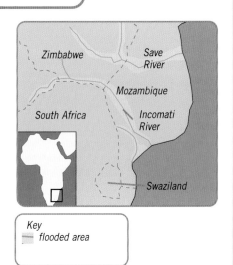

Key
─── flooded area

Case study: Boscastle flood – MEDC

Location: Boscastle, UK
Date: 16 August 2004

Causes
- Summer storms resulted in 77mm of rainfall in two hours.
- The ground was waterlogged from previous rainfall.
- Steep slopes and narrow valleys meant rainwater reached the Jordan and Valency rivers quickly causing a flash **flood**.

Effects
- 100 people had to be airlifted to safety.
- 58 properties were flooded. Cars and buildings were washed into the sea.
- People have suffered mental trauma as a result of their experiences.

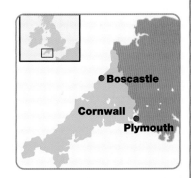

Flood control

There are a number of techniques designed to prevent, or reduce, the impact of flooding. These techniques may be divided into hard and soft strategies.

Hard strategies

Preventing floods from happening through:

- dams – built in the upper river valley, can control the discharge of the river.
- levées – increase the height of the river banks, floodwater is contained.
- straightening meanders – increases speed of river to remove flood water quickly.
- spillways – overflow channels allow river to flood low-value or unused land.
- afforestation – planting trees increases interception and evapotranspiration, reduces run-off.

Soft strategies

Helping people cope with floods through:

- flood warning systems – giving people time to remove possessions and evacuate area
- flood proofing – using sandbags, door and window sealing devices, or even building floating houses
- insurance – spreads the cost of flood damage
- zoning – prevents new building in areas at risk from flooding – in UK based on Environment Agency flood risk maps.

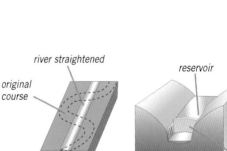

straightened meanders

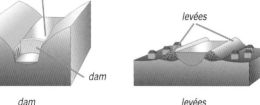

dam

levées

sandbags

Make sure you understand these terms before moving on!

- discharge
- floods
- hard strategies
- precipitation
- soft strategies

QUICK TEST

1. What type of flooding may be caused by a storm?
2. How does urbanisation increase the risk of flooding?
3. What is the difference between hard and soft river strategies?
4. What is zoning?
5. How does afforestation reduce the flood risk?

Glaciation

Glaciation is the effects large bodies of ice have on the landscape. Postglacial areas provide opportunities for farming, forestry and tourism.

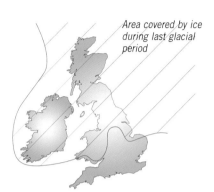

Glacial periods

- **The last glacial period (*Ice Age*) began 80 000 years ago.**
- **Ice sheets extended from the North Pole and South Pole to cover 30% of the planet.**
- **In the UK, glaciers grew as far south as South Wales, the Midlands and Norfolk.**
- **10 000 years ago the ice sheets retreated – we are now in an interglacial period.**

Area covered by ice during last glacial period

Human activity in upland glaciated areas

During interglacial periods, glaciated regions provide opportunities for people.

Case study: The French Alps

Settlement – tourist resorts such as Chamonix have developed.

Skiing – 40 000 ski runs have been developed – extensive network of chair lifts and cable cars.

Hydro-electric power (HEP) – steep slopes, high precipitation and snow melt are ideal for HEP.

Forestry – coniferous forests grow below an altitude of 1800 m. Wood is used for fuel, building and paper making.

Recreation – watersports and fishing opportunities.

Walking – dramatic scenery attracts tourists on summer walking holidays.

Farming – sheltered valley floor with deep fertile soils – suitable for dairy farming and some arable crops such as hay.

Communications – deep, straight valleys provide natural routeways for road and rail links.

Glaciers

- Glaciers are slow-moving rivers of ice that form in mountainous areas.
- Location – today glaciers are found in mountainous areas such as the Alps, Rockies and Himalayas.

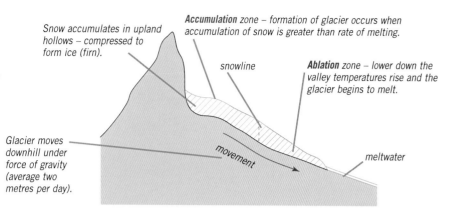

Snow accumulates in upland hollows – compressed to form ice (firn).

Accumulation zone – formation of glacier occurs when accumulation of snow is greater than rate of melting.

snowline

Ablation zone – lower down the valley temperatures rise and the glacier begins to melt.

Glacier moves downhill under force of gravity (average two metres per day).

movement

meltwater

The snowline is the point below which snow melts during the summer.

Glacier movement and erosion

As glaciers slide downhill they cause massive erosion of the land, carving out huge U-shaped valleys.

freeze-thaw – water seeps into cracks in rock on valley sides ➡ freezes ➡ expands ➡ pressure causes rock to fracture ➡ loose fragments fall onto glacier surface

abrasion – plucked rocks frozen to glacier grind away the surrounding valley.

plucking – ice melts, then freezes around rocks and 'plucks' them away as glacier moves.

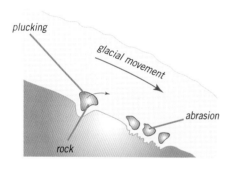

plucking

glacial movement

abrasion

rock

Issues in upland glaciated areas

The French Alps are a fragile environment which have been altered by human activity.
- The Alps receive over 100 million visitors each year.
- Deforestation of slopes for ski runs has increased the number of avalanches.
- Increase in traffic leads to air pollution.
- Walkers cause footpath erosion and trample alpine plants.
- Decline in traditional farming as young people take jobs in tourist industry.

KEY TERMS

Make sure you understand these terms before moving on!
- ablation
- abrasion
- accumulation
- freeze-thaw
- Ice Age
- plucking

QUICK TEST

1. When did the last glacial period in the UK end?
2. What happens in a glacial ablation zone?
3. What are the three processes of glacial erosion?
4. Why are the Alps suitable for HEP?
5. How has the increase in Alpine skiing led to problems?

Glacial landforms

Corries

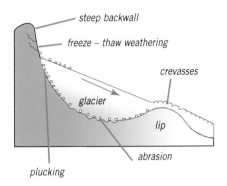

steep backwall
freeze – thaw weathering
crevasses
glacier
lip
abrasion
plucking

Case study: Stickle Tarn, Lake District

- **Corries** (also known as cirques and cwms) are deep circular hollows near mountain tops where glaciers formed – up to 2 km across.
- Formed by snow collecting in hollows ➡ compacted and turned to ice ➡ moves downhill under own weight ➡ freeze-thaw, abrasion and plucking steepen corrie sides and deepen floor.
- Lip forms at edge of corrie where there is less erosion ➡ glacier passes over lip ➡ tension in ice causes fractures called crevasses.
- Today corries often contain lakes called tarns.

Moraines

Case study: Great Langdale Valley, Lake District

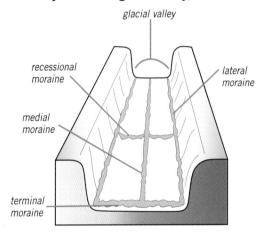

glacial valley
recessional moraine
lateral moraine
medial moraine
terminal moraine

- Glacial till is the term given to material transported and deposited by a glacier when it melts. Till is made up of sediment as small as fine clay and as large as huge boulders. **Moraines** are landforms made from till.
- Lateral moraine is deposited at the sides of the valley.
- Medial moraine is deposited in the centre of the valley – formed when two glaciers converge.
- Recessional moraine forms a line of till across the valley – formed as the glacier retreated, melting stopped for a period and further deposition occurred.
- Terminal moraine is deposited at the end of the glacier – the furthest point reached.

Glacial troughs and ribbon lakes

- **Ribbon lakes** are long narrow lakes on the valley floor of glacial valleys – also called finger lakes.
- Formed by over-deepening of valley by glacier in places ➡ increase in power where two glaciers merged or area of softer rock.
- After melting, glacial deposits may dam the valley allowing lakes to form.

When a glacier slowly flows downhill it erodes the pre-glacial river valley to form a wider and deeper U shaped valley, known as a glacial trough.

Case study: Wasdale Valley and Wastwater Lake, Lake District
As a glacier moves along its valley, changes in its size and energy may lead to increased deepening of sections of the valley floor. Areas of less-resistant rock may also be more easily eroded and deepened. When the glacier

retreats, the deepened sections fill with melt water and become ribbon lakes (finger lakes). These lakes remain long after an ice age has ended, supplied with water from streams and rivers.

Truncated spurs and hanging valleys

- **Truncated spurs** are interlocking river spurs which have been cut-off to form steep cliffs.
- Formed as glacier widened and deepened the original river valley.

Case study: Great Langdale Valley, Lake District

- A hanging valley joins the main U-shaped valley, high above its floor.
- Formed when tributary glacier joined main glacier ➡ erosive power not so great ➡ when glacier melted a sharp drop remained.
- Today rivers may descend as waterfalls from **hanging valleys**.

Case study: Little Langdale, Lake District

Drumlins

- **Drumlins** are long, narrow, egg-shaped hills formed from glacial till.
- Drumlins occur in large numbers – swarms – look like a 'basket of eggs'.
- Formation of drumlins is not fully understood.
- Deposited by glacier but then shaped while it continued moving.
- Blunt end of drumlin faces the direction from which the ice came.

Case study: Great Langdale, Valley, Lake District

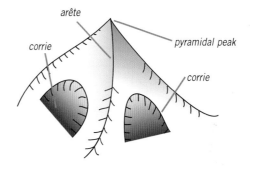

direction of glacier flow

drumlin

100 m

1.5 km

Arêtes and pyramidal peaks

- An **arête** is a steep-sided narrow ridge between two corries in a mountain area.
- Formed as the backwalls and sides of corries are weathered and eroded – distance between corries is narrowed until a knife-edge ridge is formed.

Case study: Striding Edge, Lake District

- A **pyramidal peak** is a sharp, pointed mountain summit.
- Formed when three or more corries are weathered and eroded backwards into a mountain top, until a sharp peak is created.

arête

corrie

pyramidal peak

corrie

Case study: Mt Snowdon, Wales

💡 *You may be asked to identify glacial features on an oblique aerial photograph.*

 KEY TERMS

Make sure you understand these terms before moving on!

- arêtes
- corries
- drumlins
- hanging valleys
- moraines
- pyramidal peaks
- ribbon lakes
- truncated spurs

QUICK TEST

1. Why does a lip form at the edge of a corrie?
2. What landform results where two corries meet?
3. Why are waterfalls common in upland glaciated areas?
4. What is a truncated spur?
5. How are drumlins formed?

Coastal processes

■ Coastlines are dynamic environments that are shaped by processes of erosion, transportation and deposition.

Formation of waves

Waves are caused by wind

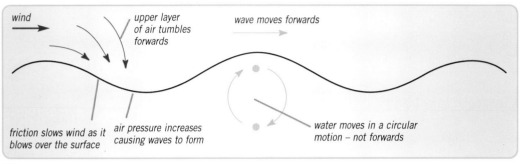

wind

upper layer of air tumbles forwards

wave moves forwards

friction slows wind as it blows over the surface

air pressure increases causing waves to form

water moves in a circular motion – not forwards

Wave energy

The size and energy of waves depends on four factors:

■ Fetch – the further wind has travelled, the larger it is.

■ Strength of wind – the stronger the wind, the larger the wave.

■ Duration of wind – the longer the wind blows, the larger the wave.

■ Offshore gradient – the steeper the offshore gradient, the larger the wave.

Remember the moon causes tides – not waves.

Types of waves

Breaking waves

■ Wave approaches shallow water ➡ lower part slowed by friction from sea bed ➡ upper part continues moving forward ➡ top of wave is unsupported and unstable ➡ wave topples forwards and breaks ➡ crashes into cliffs, or surges up a beach.

■ Swash – wave surging up a beach.

■ Backwash – wave washing back down a beach.

Destructive waves

■ Storm conditions – high winds.

■ High in proportion to length.

■ Backwash is stronger than swash.

■ Frequent waves – 11 to 15 per minute.

■ Erosion rates are high.

Constructive waves

■ Calm conditions – light winds.

■ Long in relation to height.

■ Swash is stronger than backwash.

■ Gentle waves – 6 to 9 per minute.

■ Deposition occurs.

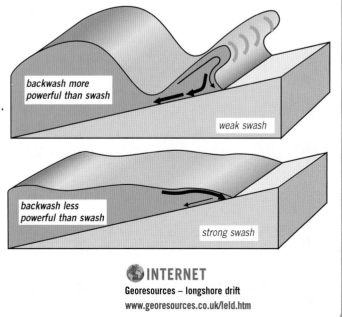

backwash more powerful than swash

weak swash

backwash less powerful than swash

strong swash

🌐 **INTERNET**
Georesources – longshore drift
www.georesources.co.uk/leld.htm

Deposition

Beach material may come from eroded cliffs, offshore sediment banks or river bedload.

- Beach material is deposited by constructive waves to form coastal landforms.
- Offshore deposition forms sandbars and gravel banks.
- Onshore **deposition** forms beaches and spits.
- Beach material is described by its size – boulders, cobbles, pebbles, sand and silt.

Erosion

The **erosion** of the coast by the sea occurs in four ways:
1. Hydraulic power – the sheer force of waves crashing against cliffs ➡ air and water trapped in cracks is compressed ➡ pressure increases ➡ rock fractures explosively.
2. Corrasion/abrasion – stones and pebbles are thrown against cliffs by breaking waves ➡ cliffs are worn away and undercut by the sandblasting effect.
3. Corrosion – sea water slowly dissolves calcium carbonate in chalk and limestone.
4. Attrition – stones and pebbles carried by waves smash into each other, breaking into smaller and rounder pieces ➡ eventually becoming sand.

Transportation

Beach material is transported up, down and along the coast in four ways:
1. Traction – boulders and cobbles are rolled along by powerful waves.
2. Saltation – pebbles are bounced along by waves.
3. Suspension – sand and silt are carried in suspension.
4. Solution – calcium carbonate and salts are dissolved in the sea water.

Longshore drift
The **transportation** of beach material along the coast by waves is called longshore drift.

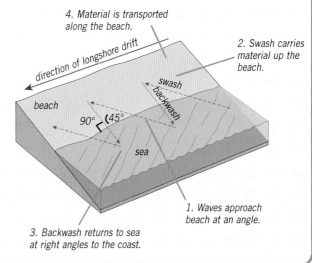

4. Material is transported along the beach.

2. Swash carries material up the beach.

direction of longshore drift

swash
backwash

beach

90° ⌐ (45°

sea

1. Waves approach beach at an angle.

3. Backwash returns to sea at right angles to the coast.

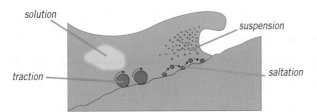

solution

suspension

traction

saltation

Make sure you understand these terms before moving on!
- constructive waves
- deposition
- destructive waves
- erosion
- longshore Drift
- transportation
- waves

QUICK TEST

1. What causes waves?
2. Which factor is the most important in controlling wave energy?
3. What type of wave occurs when swash is stronger than backwash?
4. What type of rocks are eroded by corrosion?
5. What process moves pebbles and sand along a beach?

Coastal landforms

Erosion, transportation and deposition create coastal landforms.

Headlands and bays

Headlands and **bays** are formed in areas with different rock types.

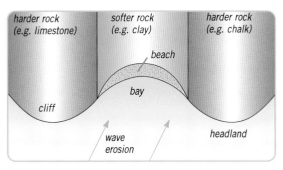

The softer rock is eroded more quickly to form bays. The harder rock forms headlands.

Case study: Swanage Dorset

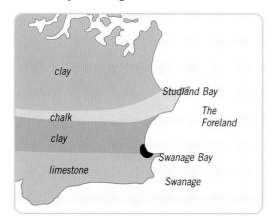

Cliffs and wave-cut platforms

- Sea **cliffs** and **wave-cut platforms** are the most widespread coastal landform. They are formed by coastal erosion.
- The rate of retreat and cliff angle will depend on the geology, e.g. granite has a slow rate of retreat and a steep angle, whereas clay retreats quickly and has gentle slopes.

7. Cliff will eventually collapse again along a slip plane.

6. New wave-cut notch eroded.

5. Collapsed cliff is eroded to form beach material.

3. Cliff becomes unstable and collapses under its own weight.

1. Waves erode and undercut base of cliff.

original cliff

2. Wave-cut notch is formed and gradually enlarged.

4. Wave-cut platform develops as cliffs retreat inland.

Beaches

Beaches are a build-up of sand, pebbles and cobbles on a wave-cut platform.

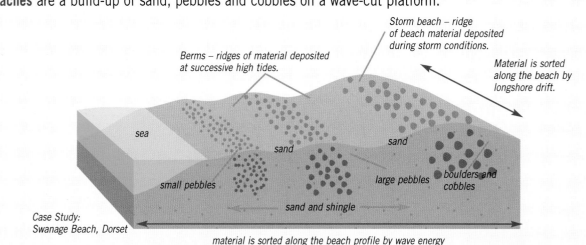

Berms – ridges of material deposited at successive high tides.

Storm beach – ridge of beach material deposited during storm conditions.

Material is sorted along the beach by longshore drift.

sea

sand

sand

small pebbles

large pebbles

boulders and cobbles

sand and shingle

Case Study: Swanage Beach, Dorset

material is sorted along the beach profile by wave energy

Spits

- **Spits** are curved beaches of sand and pebbles that extend out into the sea. They are formed by longshore drift and deposition.
- Spits are formed at a river mouth, or where the coast changes direction. They are relatively unstable and change position over time.

Case study: Spurn Head Spit, Holderness

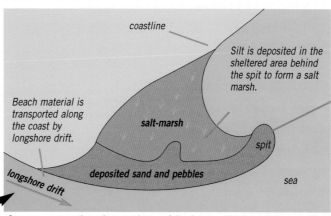

coastline

Silt is deposited in the sheltered area behind the spit to form a salt marsh.

Beach material is transported along the coast by longshore drift.

salt-marsh

Hooked end will develop if the wind sometimes blows from the other direction.

spit

deposited sand and pebbles

longshore drift

sea

prevailing wind

Over many years the spit grows longer, following the direction of the prevailing wind.

Caves, arches, stacks and stumps

Caves, **arches**, **stacks** and **stumps** are formed by the erosion of a narrow headland.

1 Faults and joints are natural areas of weakness found in rocks.
2 Cracks are formed as faults and joints are eroded by waves.
3 Caves form as the cracks are enlarged and the cliff undercut.
4 Arches form as caves grow larger and break through a headland.
5 Stacks form when the top of the arch collapses under its own weight.
6 Stumps are the remains of stacks which have collapsed.

Case Study: The Foreland, Dorset

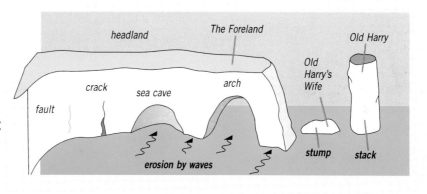

headland The Foreland Old Harry

Old Harry's Wife

crack arch

sea cave

fault

erosion by waves

stump stack

KEY TERMS

Make sure you understand these terms before moving on!

- arches
- bays
- beaches
- caves
- cliffs
- headlands
- spits
- stacks
- stumps
- wave-cut platforms

QUICK TEST

1 Which would be steeper, granite cliffs or clay cliffs?
2 What feature is formed when an arch collapses?
3 Where would you find a wave-cut notch?
4 Name two depositional coastal landforms.
5 What is formed in the sheltered area behind a spit?

Coastal management

Two important issues in coastal areas are managing coastal erosion, and managing tourism.

Coastal protection

Many coastal areas are heavily populated and have a high economic value. When areas are at risk from coastal erosion or coastal flooding a number of strategies may be used to reduce the risk.

Hard engineering strategies

- **Groynes** – wooden barriers built on the beach that jut into the sea. Groynes trap sand and pebbles being transported by longshore drift to build up the beach. The beach absorbs the impact of the waves.

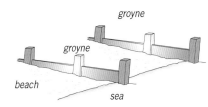

groyne
groyne
groyne
beach
sea

- Concrete **sea walls** – curved walls built at the back of the beach. The shape is designed to reflect the wave energy. Sea walls also prevent coastal flooding.

sea wall

- **Rock armour** – large boulders are placed at the base of cliffs to prevent erosion, undercutting and cliff collapse.

rock armour

- Cliff stabilisation – coastal cliffs often collapse when they become saturated with rainwater. Installing drains at the top of cliffs strengthens them by removing water quickly. Cliffs may also be graded (terraced) to make them more stable.
- Beach nourishment – beaches are the best form of coastal defence. Beach material lost by longshore drift is replaced with material dredged from the seabed.
- Gabions – boulders and cobbles are wired together in steel mesh. The stones absorb the wave energy and are prevented from moving by the wire.

gabion

Advantages
- Strategies are effective in preventing erosion and flooding.
- Beach and cliff stabilisation benefits the economy, e.g. tourism.

Disadvantages
- Strategies are expensive and have limited life.
- Preventing coastal erosion in one area makes it worse further along the coast.

Soft engineering strategies
- Managed retreat – in areas of low economic value the sea is allowed to erode and flood the land.
  Gradually mud flats, salt marshes and beaches develop, forming natural coastal defences.

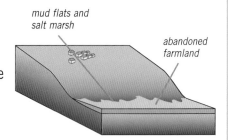

mud flats and salt marsh

abandoned farmland

Advantages
- Low-cost and long-term form of management.
- New habitats for coastal wildlife.

Disadvantages
Loss of homes, roads and farmland ➡ angry people.

Cost–benefit analysis
Coastal protection only goes ahead if the value of the land at risk exceeds the cost of the coastal defences. The cost is split between Department of Environment, Food and Rural Affairs (DEFRA) (70%) and the local authority (30%).

Coastal erosion

Case study : Holderness Coast

Location: Mappleton, Yorkshire

Problems
- Cliffs formed from soft clay called till.
- Rapid coastal erosion – up to two metres per year.
- Village of Mappleton and important coastal road at risk.

Solution

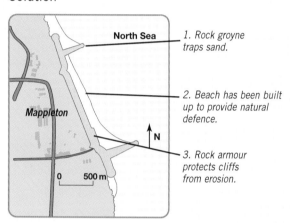

1. Rock groyne traps sand.

2. Beach has been built up to provide natural defence.

3. Rock armour protects cliffs from erosion.

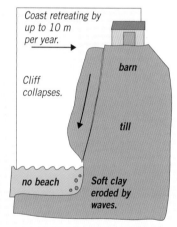

Coast retreating by up to 10 m per year.

Cliff collapses.

barn

till

no beach

Soft clay eroded by waves.

Impacts
- Groynes have reduced longshore drift and stopped coastal erosion at Mappleton. However erosion has increased to the South

Managing tourism

Case study: Scarborough, Yorkshire

Coastal environments provide opportunities for recreation and tourism. Local authorities and landowners must manage coastal areas to protect the environment and minimise conflicts between different groups of people.

Attractions
- Located close to North York Moors National Park with two sandy beaches.
- Landscaped gardens and parklands.
- Visitor attractions e.g. Atlantis Waterpark and Sea Life Centre.

Benefits of tourism
- Provides 17% of employment.
- Generates income of £250–£300 million per year.
- Locals have access to tourist facilities.

Problems with tourism
- Decline in visitor numbers due to overseas competition.
- Seasonal nature of tourism results in unemployment in winter.

Managing tourism
- New markets such as business conferences developed.
- Tourist season extended with festivals and cheap breaks.
- New sewage outfall to remove sewage.

KEY TERMS

Make sure you understand these terms before moving on!
- groynes
- hard engineering
- rock armour
- sea walls
- soft engineering

QUICK TEST

1. How do groynes protect the coast from erosion?
2. Why do sea walls often have a curved shape?
3. What is 'managed retreat'?
4. Who pays for coastal protection schemes?
5. Why might coastal defences in one area increase erosion elsewhere?

Weather

Weather means the atmospheric conditions at a certain place and time.

Weather components

- Temperature – how hot or cold the air is.
- Air pressure – weight of the atmosphere.
- Wind – horizontal movement of air.
- Clouds – water droplets or ice crystals held in the atmosphere.
- Relative humidity – actual amount of water vapour in the air relative to the maximum that could be held.
- Precipitation – deposition of water from the atmosphere as rain, hail, snow and sleet.

 All weather is powered by energy from the Sun.

Rainfall

There are three types of rainfall

Convectional rainfall
Convectional rainfall only happens when it is hot.

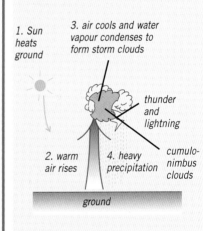

1. Sun heats ground

3. air cools and water vapour condenses to form storm clouds

thunder and lightning

2. warm air rises

4. heavy precipitation

cumulo-nimbus clouds

ground

Frontal rainfall
Frontal rainfall happens when warm air and cool air meet.

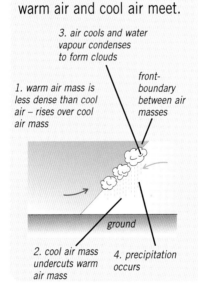

3. air cools and water vapour condenses to form clouds

front-boundary between air masses

1. warm air mass is less dense than cool air – rises over cool air mass

ground

2. cool air mass undercuts warm air mass

4. precipitation occurs

Relief rainfall
Relief rainfall happens when moist air rises over hills and mountains.

2. air cools and water vapour condenses to form clouds

3. precipitation occurs on the hills

5. rain shadow – air is dry so very little rain falls

1. moist air is forced to rise

hill

4. dry air descends and warms up – clouds evaporate

Satellite images

Satellite images are photos taken by satellites orbiting the Earth.

- Satellite images allow meteorologists to forecast the weather more accurately.

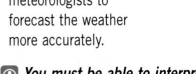 *You must be able to interpret synoptic charts and satellite images.*

Mid latitude depression (low pressure)

Tropical low pressure

Anticyclone (high pressure)

Weather systems

Anticyclones

Anticyclones are air masses of high pressure.

- Cool air sinks ➡ as it sinks it warms up (opposite to air rising) ➡ warm air can hold more water vapour and therefore clouds are much less likely to form, leading to clear dry weather.
- Summer anticyclones = light winds, sunshine and high temperatures.
- Winter anticyclones = light winds, sunshine, low temperatures and frost.
- Winds blow clockwise in Northern Hemisphere (anticlockwise in Southern).

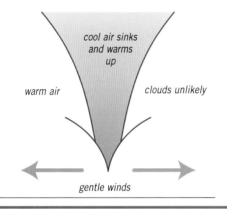

cool air sinks and warms up

warm air   clouds unlikely

gentle winds

Depressions

Depressions are areas of low pressure formed when a warm air mass and cool air mass meet.

- Warm air rises over cool air to form a warm front.
- Cool air undercuts warm air from behind to form a cold front.
- Warm air rises along both fronts, cools, condenses and forms rain.
- An occluded front is formed when warm air is completely undercut by the cool air.
- Air rises at the centre of a depression and draws in anticlockwise winds (in Northern Hemisphere). The lower the air pressure, the faster the winds.

Sequence of weather associated with the passage of a depression

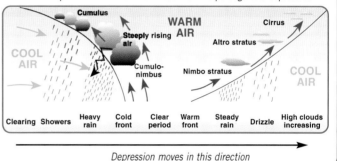

Cumulus   WARM AIR   Cirrus
Steeply rising air   Altro stratus
COOL AIR   Cumulo-nimbus   Nimbo stratus   COOL AIR

Clearing | Showers | Heavy rain | Cold front | Clear period | Warm front | Steady rain | Drizzle | High clouds increasing

Depression moves in this direction

Synoptic charts

- **Synoptic charts** are maps that summarise weather data for a particular time.
- Data for precipitation, temperature, cloud cover, wind speed, wind direction, fronts and air pressure are represented by symbols.

Temperature is shown by numbers (°C).

Wind direction shown by a line symbol.

Cloud cover is shown by shaded circles (oktas).

29
high
1028 25
1024 26
1020

Wind speed shown by feathers (knots).

low
980
984
988
992
996

FRONTS
warm front
cold front
occluded front

Isobars – lines drawn between places of equal air pressure (millibars).

Symbols are used to show the type of precipitation.

KEY TERMS

Make sure you understand these terms before moving on!
- anticyclones
- convectional rainfall
- depressions
- frontal rainfall
- relief rainfall
- satellite images
- synoptic charts

QUICK TEST

1. Is high pressure caused by rising or sinking air?
2. Why is the sheltered side of a hill called the rain shadow?
3. What time of the year does convectional rainfall occur in the UK?
4. What weather conditions would you expect in a winter anticyclone?
5. What direction does the wind blow in a depression in the UK?

Climate

Climate is the average weather of a place based on data recorded over a 30-year period.

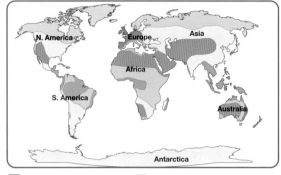

continental interior – hot in summer, cold in winter, wettest in summer

temperate maritime – moderate temperatures and rain all year; influenced by the sea

tundra – short summer, long cold winter

tropical – equatorial climate; hot and wet all year

hot deserts – hot with very little rain

Mediterranean – hot dry summers, mild wet winters

tropical grassland – hot all year with a wet season and a dry season

🌐 **INTERNET**
World Climate data
http://www.worldclimate.com/

Factors affecting climate

Latitude

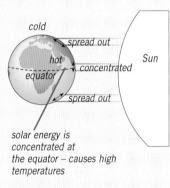

cold

spread out

hot

equator

concentrated

Sun

spread out

solar energy is concentrated at the equator – causes high temperatures

towards the North and South poles solar energy is more spread out causes cold temperatures

- Latitude is how far north or south a place is from the equator

Altitude

- Altitude is the height above sea level – the higher a place is the colder and wetter it will be.

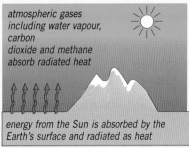

density of atmosphere decreases with altitude and absorbs less heat

atmospheric gases including water vapour, carbon dioxide and methane absorb radiated heat

atmosphere is densest at Earth's surface and absorbs the most heat

energy from the Sun is absorbed by the Earth's surface and radiated as heat

temperature decreases with altitude

factors affecting climate

Distance from sea

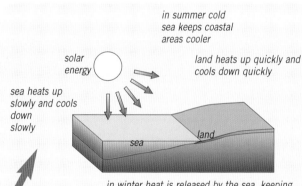

in summer cold sea keeps coastal areas cooler

solar energy

land heats up quickly and cools down quickly

sea heats up slowly and cools down slowly

sea

land

in winter heat is released by the sea, keeping coastal areas warmer than inland

- Places that are influenced by sea temperature have a maritime climate – wet with a small temperature range.
- Places inland that are not influenced by sea temperatures have a continental climate – dry with a large **temperature** range.

Prevailing wind

- Prevailing winds are the most frequent winds affecting an area – they influence temperature and **precipitation**.
- Sea winds bring precipitation.
- Land winds bring dry weather.
- Polar winds bring cold weather.
- Tropical winds bring warm or hot weather.

Case study: UK – temperate maritime climate

- **Climate** is moderated by influence of sea.
- Warm, wet summers – mild, wet winters.
- Dominated by mid-latitude depressions, where tropical and polar air masses meet.

Climate graphs combine average monthly temperatures (line) and average monthly precipitation (bars) – you must be able to describe and explain them.

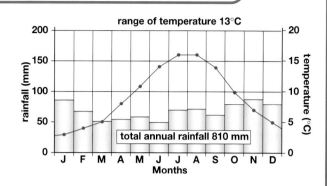

range of temperature 13°C

total annual rainfall 810 mm

January temperatures

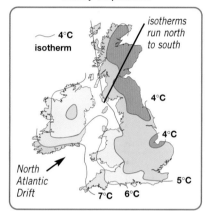

~ 4°C isotherm

isotherms run north to south

4°C

4°C

North Atlantic Drift

5°C

7°C 6°C

temperatures influenced by warm ocean current (North Atlantic Drift)

July temperatures

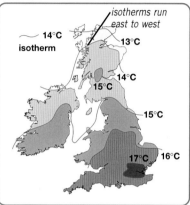

~ 14°C isotherm

isotherms run east to west

13°C

14°C

15°C

15°C

17°C 16°C

temperatures influenced by latitude (distance from equator)

Annual precipitation

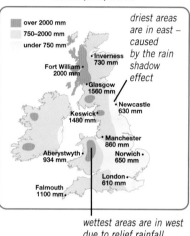

over 2000 mm
750–2000 mm
under 750 mm

driest areas are in east – caused by the rain shadow effect

- Inverness 730 mm
- Fort William 2000 mm
- Glasgow 1560 mm
- Newcastle 630 mm
- Keswick 1480 mm
- Manchester 860 mm
- Aberystwyth 934 mm
- Norwich 650 mm
- London 610 mm
- Falmouth 1100 mm

wettest areas are in west due to relief rainfall

Case study: Russia – continental interior climate

- High annual temperature range – land heats quickly in summer (average 18 °C) but loses heat quickly in winter (–19 °C).
- No moderating influence on temperatures by the sea.
- Precipitation is low due to distance from sea – average 500 mm per year.
- Maximum precipitation occurs in summer due to convectional rainfall ➡ thunderstorms and hailstones.

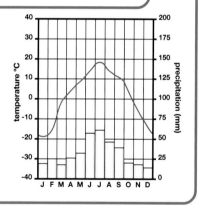

KEY TERMS

Make sure you understand these terms before moving on!
- altitude
- climate
- climate graphs
- latitude
- ocean currents
- precipitation
- prevailing wind
- temperature

QUICK TEST

1. What is the difference between weather and climate?
2. Why is it so cold at the North Pole?
3. Why do temperatures decrease with altitude?
4. What is a meant by 'maritime climate'?
5. Why are inland areas hotter than coastal areas in summer?

Weather and people

Weather and climate have a powerful influence on people's everyday lives. Weather affects the types of houses people live in, the activities of farmers and industries, and even events such as sports fixtures. Extreme weather conditions can create hazards for people, for example, tropical storms, tornadoes, snow, fog and drought.

Tropical storms

- **Tropical storms** are huge depressions that form over oceans in the tropics when sea temperature exceeds 27°C. They form in late summer/autumn and are known as **hurricanes**, cyclones and **typhoons**.
- Tropical storms may grow to over 500 km across and last seven to 14 days.
- Tropical storms move slowly away from the equator in a westerly direction.
- Powerful winds destroy buildings, power lines, telephone lines and crops.
- Heavy rainfall causes severe damage through flooding and landslides.
- Intense low pressure causes sea to rise by over five metres ➡ **storm surge** and flooding of coastal areas.
- Tropical storms will decay when they reach land because they are cut off from their power source – the warm sea.

eye of the storm – air slowly sinks resulting in gentle wind and no rain

hurricane rotates

condensation releases heat adding power to the storm

winds blow outwards at the top of the storm forming a cloud canopy

canopy

air is drawn in from the sides causing winds up to 190 kph

clouds

eye

gentle winds

water vapour rises, cools, condenses and falls as heavy rain

strong winds

intense low pressure develops as air rises

heat from sun warms sea to around 27°C

sea water evaporates to form water vapour

INTERNET
National Hurricane Center – USA
http://www.nhc.noaa.gov/

Case study: Hurricane Katrina

Location: Louisiana, USA
Date: August 2005

Effects of Hurricane Katrina

6m high **storm surge** breached flood defences
80% of city of New Orleans flooded
10 000 people sought refuge in the Superdome Stadium
City eventually completely evacuated
972 deaths
Cost of damage $75 billion (estimate)

30 August – downgraded to tropical depression

29 August – Hurricane makes landfall with winds of 125 mph

28 August – Hurricane Katrina swings northwards as winds reach 175 mph

Hurricane Katrina

© BBC.co.uk

TN

AR

MS

AL

GA

Jackson

TX

LA

Mobile

Biloxi

FL

New Orleans

Gulf of Mexico

Miami

Bahamas

Cuba

- - - **Path of Storm**
Hurricane
Tropical storm

25 August – winds reach 75 mph storm named Hurricane Katrina

23 August – Hurricane Centre (USA) reports formation of tropical depression

Drought

Causes of drought

A **drought** is a long, continuous period of dry weather. One-third of the world's population live in areas sometimes affected by drought.

- In an area of high pressure (anticyclone) warm air can hold more water vapour
- Deforestation reduces evapotranspiration ➡ no clouds ➡ no rain
- Increased demand for water caused by population growth and economic development

- Industry – water used in manufacturing (54%)
- Agriculture – irrigation for crops (33%)
- Domestic – water for homes (13%)

(Figures are an estimate of global water use.)

Impacts of drought

- Crops fail due to lack of water.
- Cattle die due to lack of food.
- **Soil erosion** occurs due to overgrazing.
- Food and water shortages lead to malnutrition, famine and death.

- Migration from rural areas increases pressures on towns.
- Economies suffer due to reduction in exports.

💡 *The peak demand for water is usually at the time of lowest supply.*

Case study: Drought in the Sahel

The Sahel is a narrow belt of semi-arid land south of the Sahara Desert in North Africa. The region only receives one to two months of rainfall each year, and this is unreliable. Since 1968 the rains have frequently failed, or been below average. This has resulted in many severe droughts.

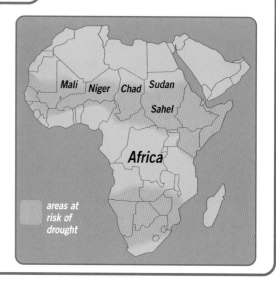

Mali Niger Chad Sudan

Sahel

Africa

areas at risk of drought

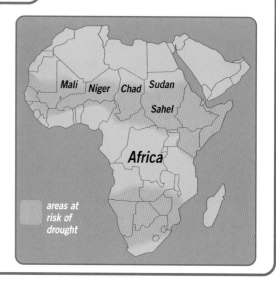
KEY TERMS

Make sure you understand these terms before moving on!

- drought
- hurricanes
- soil erosion
- storm surge
- tropical storms
- typhoons

QUICK TEST

1. At what time of year do tropical storms develop?
2. Which areas are at risk from tropical storms?
3. What happens in a storm surge?
4. What is a drought?
5. What is the physical cause of drought?

Ecosystems

■ An ecosystem is a community of trees, plants, animals and insects living in a particular environment.

■ The living organisms (*biomass*) in an ecosystem are linked together and depend on the land, water and air for their survival.

Global distribution of ecosystems

Over thousands of years, trees, plants, animals and insects have adapted to different climatic conditions around the world. Differences in sunlight, temperature and rainfall have resulted in the evolution of eight different types of **ecosystem**.

■ Tropical rainforest – hundreds of different species of tree; some trees are over 50 m tall.
■ Tropical grassland – drought-resistant trees with waxy leaves and thorns; grasses up to five metres tall.
■ Desert – drought-resistant plants, such as cacti, with very long roots to reach deep water supplies.

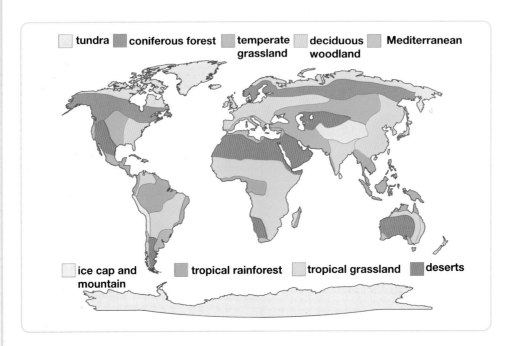

tundra   coniferous forest   temperate grassland   deciduous woodland   Mediterranean

ice cap and mountain   tropical rainforest   tropical grassland   deserts

Notice how the same types of ecosystem are found on similar lines of latitude.

■ Mediterranean – evergreen woodland, such as cork and pine; thorny shrubs with thin waxy leaves.
■ Temperate grassland – grasses up to two metres tall; some trees, such as willow.
■ Deciduous woodland – trees that shed their leaves in winter, such as oak and ash; shrubs and short grasses.
■ Coniferous forest – dense evergreen trees, such as fir and pine; few other species.
■ Tundra – short plants, such as moss, heather and lichen; some stunted trees.

The map shows the vegetation that would be growing if people had not cut it down.

Tropical grasslands

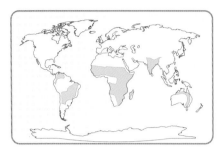

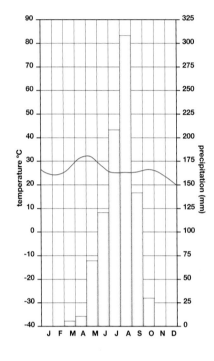

Location
- Areas include central Africa, South America and Northern Australia.

Climate
- High temperatures throughout year – average 25°C.
- Wet and dry seasons – rainfall when sun is overhead (convectional rainfall).

Soil
- Red clay

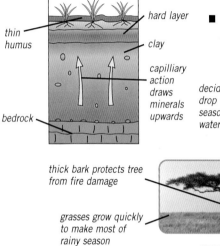

thin humus
hard layer
clay
capilliary action draws minerals upwards
bedrock

Vegetation
- Tropical grassland is a transitional area of **vegetation** between tropical rainforest and desert.
- Mixture of trees and grasses.

Human interaction
- Tropical grasslands are most suitable for nomadic pastoralism – grazing animals such as cattle or sheep.
- Crops can be grown, including tobacco, maize and millet.
- Over-cultivation causes **soil** erosion and desertification.

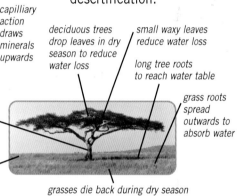

deciduous trees drop leaves in dry season to reduce water loss
small waxy leaves reduce water loss
long tree roots to reach water table
grass roots spread outwards to absorb water
thick bark protects tree from fire damage
grasses grow quickly to make most of rainy season
grasses die back during dry season

Desertification

- A desert has less than 250 mm of precipitation per year.
- Desertification is the spread of desert-like conditions into dry grassland areas.
- Every year 12 million hectares of land are becoming desert.

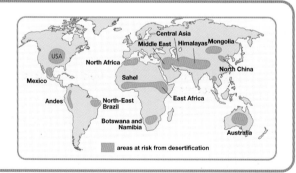

USA
Mexico
Andes
North Africa
Sahel
North-East Brazil
Botswana and Namibia
Middle East
Central Asia
Himalayas
Mongolia
North China
East Africa
Australia

areas at risk from desertification

KEY TERMS

Make sure you understand these terms before moving on!
- biomass
- climate
- ecosystem
- soil
- vegetation

QUICK TEST

1. Which key factors influence the evolution of ecosystems?
2. Describe the vegetation found in a deciduous woodland ecosystem?
3. Where are tropical grasslands found?
4. How are tropical grasses adapted to their environment?
5. How are tropical grasslands traditionally used by people?

Global environments

Tropical rainforests

Location
- **Tropical rainforests** are located 5° North and South of the equator.
- Areas include Brazil, West Africa and South-East Asia.

Soil
- Red clay

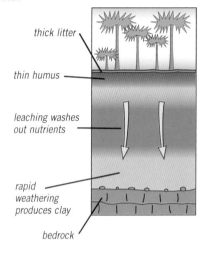

thick litter

thin humus

leaching washes out nutrients

rapid weathering produces clay

bedrock

Climate
- High temperatures all year – average 27°C.
- High humidity, resulting in daily convectional rainfall.

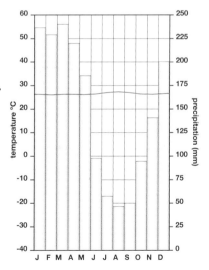

Vegetation
- One hectare of rainforest may contain 500 different species of tree and over 1000 different types of plant.
- Trees have buttress roots to support great height, and leaves have drip tips to shed heavy rainfall.
- **Vegetation** is divided into five layers.

Human interaction
Tropical rainforests are at risk of **deforestation** for the following reasons:
- Agriculture – forest cleared to provide farmland.
- Settlement – land is needed to provide homes.
- Ranching – forest is cleared to graze cattle.
- Logging – timber is exported.
- Mining – gold, iron ore and bauxite are mined.
- Dams – built to provide hydro- electricity.

Effects of deforestation
- Soil erosion occurs due to heavy rainfall on exposed soil → soil silts up rivers.
- Infertile soil results in crop failure for new farmers after only three or four harvests.
- Rare plants, animals and insects will become extinct, and we will lose potentially life saving medicines.
- Indigenous forest people are losing their homes and culture.
- Deforestation will increase amount of CO_2 in atmosphere and contribute to climate change.

Sustainable management
Sustainable management of tropical rainforests is possible by:
- Selective felling of valuable mature trees only.
- Transporting harvested logs by helicopter rather than road.
- Harvesting valuable products such as Brazil nuts to provide a long term income.
- People living in MEDCs buying only timber approved by the Forest Stewardship Council (FSC).

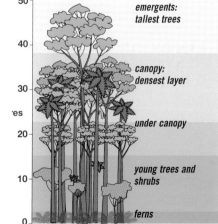

emergents: tallest trees

canopy: densest layer

under canopy

young trees and shrubs

ferns

Coniferous forests

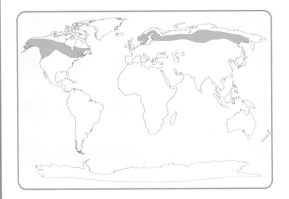

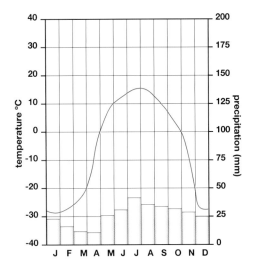

Location
- Areas include Northern Europe, Siberia, USA and Canada.

Climate
- Long winters with temperatures as low as –30°C.
- Low precipitation as cold dry air is unable to hold moisture.

Soil
- Podsol

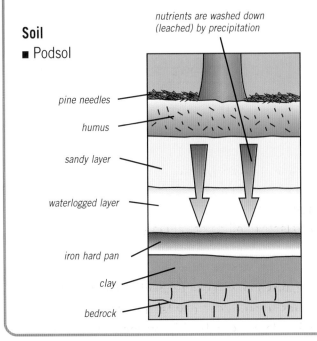

nutrients are washed down (leached) by precipitation

pine needles
humus
sandy layer
waterlogged layer
iron hard pan
clay
bedrock

Vegetation
- **Coniferous forest** consists of trees such as spruce, fir and pine.
- Few species at ground level due to lack of light and layer of needles.

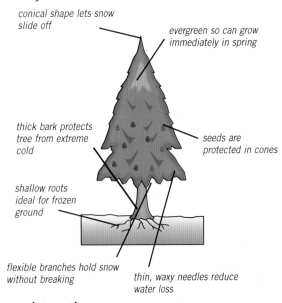

conical shape lets snow slide off

evergreen so can grow immediately in spring

thick bark protects tree from extreme cold

seeds are protected in cones

shallow roots ideal for frozen ground

flexible branches hold snow without breaking

thin, waxy needles reduce water loss

Human interaction
- Coniferous trees are felled to provide softwood timber and wood pulp for making paper.

KEY TERMS

Make sure you understand these terms before moving on!
- coniferous forests
- deforestation
- sustainable management
- tropical rainforest
- vegetation

QUICK TEST

1. How are coniferous trees adapted to their environment?
2. What type of soil occurs in coniferous forests?
3. Where are tropical rainforest ecosystems located?
4. Describe the tropical rainforest climate.
5. How are tropical rainforest trees adapted to their environment?

Map skills

All exam boards require you to be able to interpret maps.

Direction and scale

- **Direction** is given using the points of a compass..
- The top of the map is nearly always North.
- Ordnance Survey (OS) maps have light-blue grid lines running from North to South and from East to West.
- Scale tells you how much smaller a map is compared to real life.
- On a 1:50 000 map, 2 cm are equal to 1 km.
- On a 1:25 000 map, 4 cm are equal to 1 km.

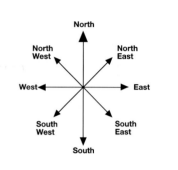

Grid references

Four-figure grid references

Four-figure grid references locate an area of 1 km^2.

1. Move along the bottom of the map until you come to the first two numbers.
2. Move up the side of the map, until you come to the second two numbers.
3. Follow the two lines until they meet.
4. This point forms the corner of four grid squares.
5. The correct grid square is the one above, and to the right, of that point.

Six-figure grid references

Six-figure grid references locate an area of 100 m^2.

1. Move along the bottom of the map until you come to the first two numbers.
2. To find the third number, imagine the next square is divided into 10 small parts.
3. Move along until you come to about the right place.
4. Move up the side of the map until you find the fourth and fifth numbers.
5. To find the sixth number, again imagine the next square is divided into 10.
6. Follow the two lines until they meet.
7. This point is the exact six-figure grid reference.

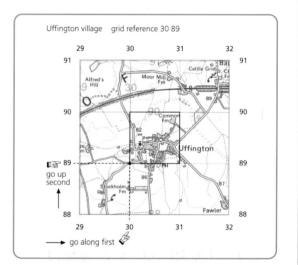

Uffington village   grid reference 30 89

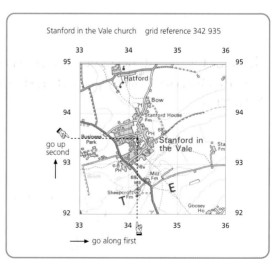

Stanford in the Vale church   grid reference 342 935

INTERNET
Ordnance Survey
http://www.ordnancesurvey.co.uk/

Relief

- **Relief** means the shape and height of the land – make your examiner happy by learning this!
- The clearest way of showing relief on a map is with **contour lines**.
- Contours are thin brown lines that join all places at the same height above sea level.
- Numbers written along contour lines show height in metres.
- Contours usually increase in 10 m intervals, but be careful, as this does vary.
- The closer together the contour lines, the steeper the slope.

Heights are also shown by spot heights (below left) and triangulation points (below right).

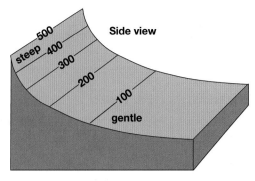

Side view

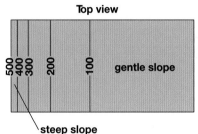

Top view

gentle slope

steep slope

• 364   **364 metres above sea level**

△ 678   **678 metres above sea level**

Measuring distance

- You will probably be asked to measure the **distance** between two places on a map.
- The easiest way to do this is with a piece of paper (use the edge of your exam paper if you need to), as follows:
1. Place a piece of paper on the map, between the two places you want to measure.
2. Mark the two places onto the paper with arrows.
3. Put the piece of paper along the scale at the bottom of the map.
4. Read off the distance using the scale.

- To measure distances that are not in a straight line, mark off a piece of paper in small sections.
- Do not use a ruler to work out distance – it is too easy to make mistakes converting centimetres into kilometres.

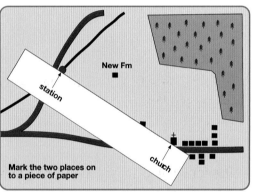

Mark the two places on to a piece of paper

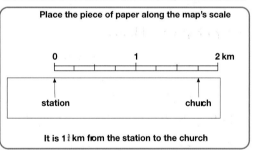

Place the piece of paper along the map's scale

It is 1¾ km from the station to the church

 Remember – whatever the scale of OS maps, one grid square always represents 1 km².

KEY TERMS

Make sure you understand these terms before moving on!
- contour lines
- direction
- distance
- four-figure grid references
- relief
- six-figure grid references

QUICK TEST

❶ How many centimetres equal 1 km on a 1 : 25000 map?

❷ Which shows more detail, a 1 : 50000 map, or a 1 : 25000 map?

❸ How large an area is covered by a four-figure grid reference?

❹ What is at 337929 in Stanford in the Vale?

❺ How is height shown on OS maps?

Practice questions

Use the questions to test
your progress.
Check your answers on page 93.

Tectonic Activity

1. Is the volcano in Figure 1 a shield volcano or a composite volcano? (1 mark)

   composite

A *crater*

B *magma chamber*

C *vent*

Figure 1

2. Label features A, B and C on Figure 1. (3 marks)

3. Describe how a composite volcano is formed. (4 marks)

   on a destructive plate boundary. The magma forces it's way up through the continental plate as the oceanic plate is pushed into the subduction zone and melted

4. Name two hazards caused by volcanic eruptions. (2 marks)

   pyroclastic flow, ashfall

5. Why do earthquakes and volcanoes happen in the same locations? (2 marks)

   because they both ~~occur~~ are caused by different types of plate boundaries and occur on fault lines of these boundaries

6. Explain the cause of an earthquake you have studied. (4 marks)

   Kobe earthquake was caused by the Eurasian continental plate and the philipines oceanic plate on their destructive plate boundary. The Philipines plate got pushed under the Eurasion plate and the pressure as the plates moved caused an Earthquake.

7. Why do people live in areas at risk of earthquakes and volcanic eruptions? (6 marks)

   There are advantages such as fertile land and soil from the weathered ash and lava. Minerals such as gold and diamonds are found in volcanic areas and tourism often thrives with people coming to see geysers and bubbling mud pools.

8. Name a range of fold mountains you have studied. (1 mark)

   The Alps

9. Give two ways in which people use fold mountain areas. (2 marks)

   Settlement
   Tourism, e.g. skiing

Rocks and Landscapes

1. Is granite an igneous, sedimentary or metamorphic rock? (1 mark)

    ....

2. Give two characteristics of sedimentary rocks. (2 marks)

    ....

    ....

3. Describe the formation of metamorphic rocks. (3 marks)

    ....

    ....

    ....

4. Name the process of weathering shown in Figure 2. (1 mark)

    ....

    ....

Figure 2

5. Explain the process of weathering shown in Figure 2. (4 marks)

    ....

    ....

    ....

6. Explain the formation of limestone pavements. (4 marks)

    ....

    ....

    ....

7. Describe the human uses of limestone areas. (4 marks)

    ....

    ....

    ....

8. Describe the characteristics of a granite landscape that you have studied. (6 marks)

    ....

    ....

    ....

    ....

    ....

    ....

/50

How well did you do?   ✗ 1-12 Start again   13-26 Getting there   27-38 Good work   39-50 Excellent! ✓

Practice questions

Use the questions to test your progress.
Check your answers on pages 93–4.

River Landscapes

1. Label features A, B and C on Figure 1. (3 marks)

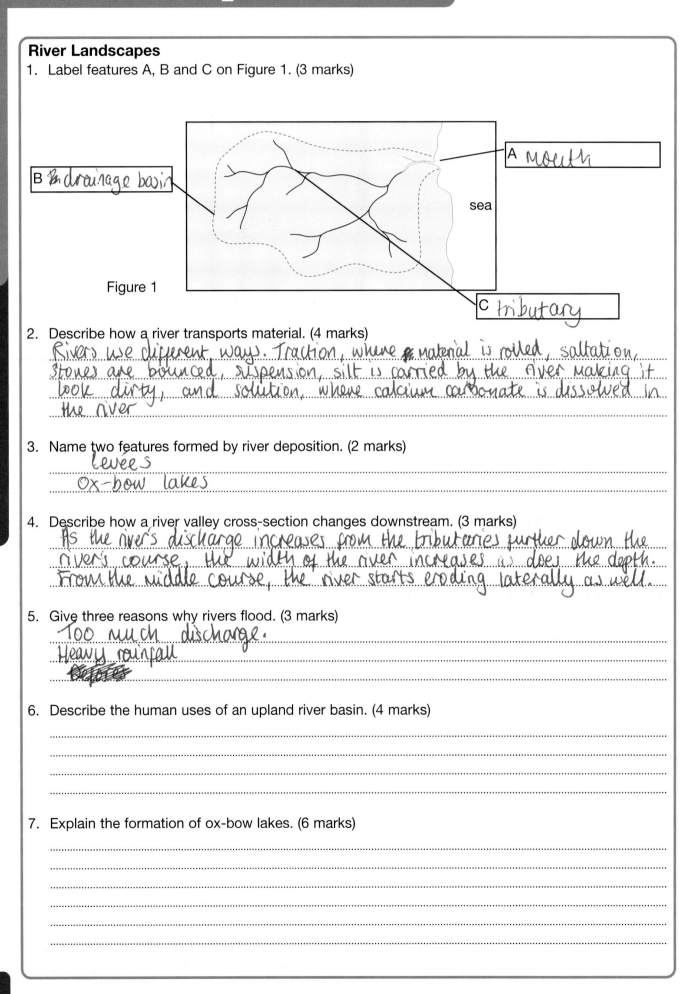

B ~~Th~~ drainage basin

A mouth

sea

Figure 1

C tributary

2. Describe how a river transports material. (4 marks)

Rivers use different ways. Traction, where material is rolled, saltation, stones are bounced, suspension, silt is carried by the river making it look dirty, and solution, where calcium carbonate is dissolved in the river

3. Name two features formed by river deposition. (2 marks)

Levees
Ox-bow lakes

4. Describe how a river valley cross-section changes downstream. (3 marks)

As the river's discharge increases from the tributaries further down the river's course, the width of the river increases as does the depth. From the middle course, the river starts eroding laterally as well.

5. Give three reasons why rivers flood. (3 marks)

Too much discharge.
Heavy rainfall
~~Before~~

6. Describe the human uses of an upland river basin. (4 marks)

....
....
....
....

7. Explain the formation of ox-bow lakes. (6 marks)

....
....
....
....
....
....
....

Glacial Landscapes

1. Label features A, B and C on Figure 1. (3 marks)

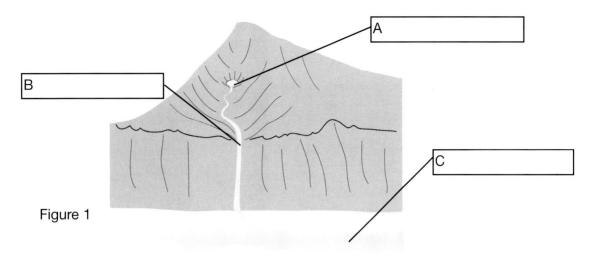

A

B

C

Figure 1

2. Describe how a glacier erodes. (4 marks)

....

....

....

3. Explain how feature A on Figure 1 was formed. (6 marks)

....

....

....

....

4. Describe the material which forms moraines. (2 marks)

....

....

5. Explain how medial moraine is formed. (2 marks)

....

....

6. Describe how people use upland glaciated areas. (4 marks)

....

....

....

7. How are upland glaciated areas managed to reduce the impacts of tourism? (4 marks)

....

....

....

/50

PRACTICE QUESTIONS

Physical geography

Practice questions

Use the questions to test
your progress.
Check your answers on page 94.

Coastal Landscapes

1. What type of waves are formed by light winds? (1 mark)

constructive

2. Label features A, B and C on Figure 2. (3 marks)

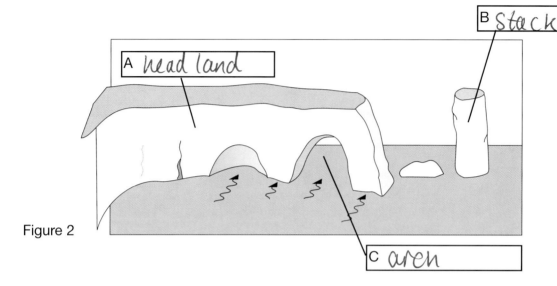

B *stack*

A *head land*

C *arch*

Figure 2

3. How do waves erode the coastline? (4 marks)

By corrosion – sea water dissolves the calcium carbonate in chalk/limestone
~~Attrition to~~ Corrasion – rocks and pebbles hitting the side of the cliff etc
Hydraulic Action – Force of the waves hitting the cliffs

4. Explain how feature B on Figure 2 was formed. (6 marks)

The ~~roc~~ top of the arch collapsed under it's own wait after being made
from erosion by the waves. It would have originally been a fault, then
a crack, then a cave, then an arch. After the arch collapses, a
stack, figure B, is ~~so~~ left.

5. Name two coastal features formed by coastal deposition. (2 marks)

Beach, spit

6. Name two methods of coastal protection. (2 marks)

Groynes, gabions

7. Explain the process of longshore drift. (3 marks)

Constructive waves with big swash ~~to~~ deposit material on the beach. The
backwash then brings some material back with it at a 90° angle to the
beach, no matter what angle the wave swash was at. This causes the beach
to move.

8. *Describe* how people use coasts. (4 marks)

Tourism.

Weather and Climate

1. Name the type of weather system shown in Figure 2. (1 mark)

....

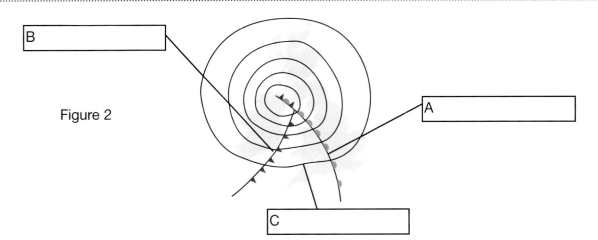

B ☐
Figure 2
A ☐
C ☐

2. Label features A, B and C on Figure 2. (3 marks)

3. Describe the type of weather experienced by the UK during a winter anticyclone. (4 marks)

....
....
....

4. What type of rainfall is occurring over town A? (1 mark)

....

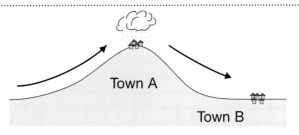

Town A

Town B

5. Explain why town B receives less rainfall than town A. (4 marks).

....
....
....

6. Explain why it is hotter at the equator than at the North Pole. (4 marks)

....

7. Describe a typical equatorial climate. (2 marks)

....

8. Describe how a tropical storm might affect peoples' lives. (6 marks)

....
....
....
....

/50

Practice questions

Use the questions to test your progress.
Check your answers on page 94.

Ecosystems

1. What is an ecosystem? (1 mark)

....

2. Describe the location of coniferous forests shown in Figure 1. (2 marks)

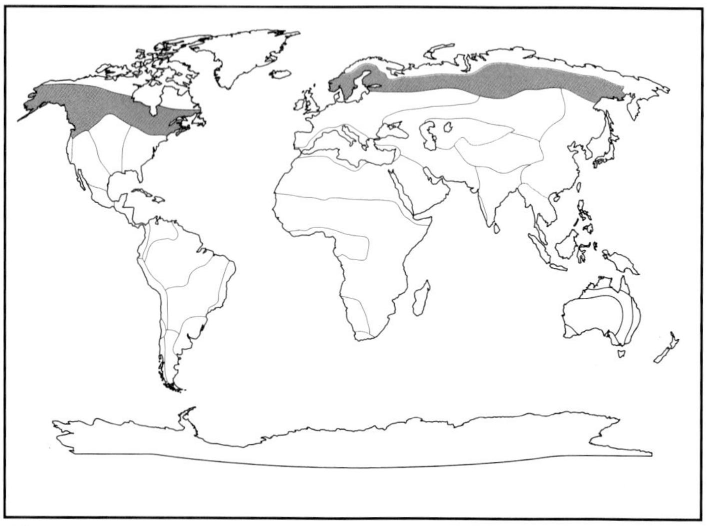

....

....

....

Figure 1

3. Name the type of soil found beneath coniferous forests. (1 mark)

....

4. Explain how the soil becomes 'leached'. (2 marks)

....

....

5. Label Figure 2 to show how coniferous trees are adapted to their environment. (4 marks)

6. Name an area of tropical rainforests you have studied. (1 mark)

....

....

Figure 2

7. Describe three reasons why tropical rainforests are being cut down. (3 x 2 marks)

....

....

....

....

8. Describe the climate of tropical grassland. (3 marks)

....

....

....

....

....

9. Explain how trees in tropical grassland are adapted to the environment. (5 marks)

....

....

....

....

....

Geographical Skills

1. Name the symbol found at 975463. (Please refer to map on page 92). (1 mark)

....

2. What is the general direction of the railway from Minehead to the edge of the map extract? (1 mark)

....

3. What is the length of the railway from Minehead station to the edge of the map extract? (2 marks)

....

4. What is the length of the secondary road that follows the coastline at Minehead, between 968473 and 984464? (2 marks)

....

5. What is the six figure grid reference for the youth hostel at Hagley? (2 marks)

....

6. What is the height of the castle mound at Dunster? (2 marks)

....

7. What is the evidence that Minehead is a tourist destination? (3 marks)

....
....
....
....
....
....

8. Describe the land use in grid square 9845. (4 marks)

....
....
....
....
....
....

9. Compare the relief in grid squares 9945 and 9743 (4 marks)

....
....
....
....
....

10. Suggest why there is little settlement to the east of Minehead. (4 marks)

....
....
....
....

/50

How well did you do?   X 1-12 Start again   13-26 Getting there   27-38 Good work   39-50 Excellent! ✓

Population

The population of the world is spread out very unevenly. During the last 200 years the world's population has increased dramatically.

Population distribution

- **Population distribution** describes how people are spread out. The **population** of the world is spread out very unevenly.
- Most people are living on only one-third of the Earth's land surface.
- Areas with high populations include Western Europe, India and China.
- Areas with low populations include Canada, North Africa, Brazil and Australia.
- Population distribution is usually shown using a dot map.

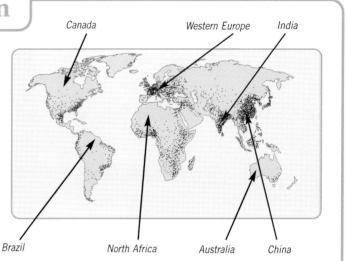

Population density

- **Population density** describes how crowded an area is. It is calculated by dividing the total population of a place by its area.

$$\frac{\text{population}}{\text{area (km}^2)} = \text{Population density (km}^2)$$

- **Densely populated** means crowded – over 50 people per km^2.
- **Sparsely populated** means few people – less than 10 people per km^2.
- Population density is usually shown using a choropleth (shaded) map.

Population Density	
area	people per km^2
World	43
UK	237
Australia	2
USA	33
China	140
India	363

The UK is one of the most densely populated countries in the world.

people per km^2

- above 50
- 10 to 50
- fewer than 10

Explaining population distribution

Several factors explain the world's population distribution and density. Positive factors encourage people to live in an area; negative factors discourage people from living in an area.

EXPLAINING POPULATION DISTRIBUTION		
Factor	Positive	Negative
Relief	Flat land	Mountainous land
Climate	Warm, enough rain	Very hot, very cold, too dry
Vegetation	Open grassland	Dense forest
Soils	Deep fertile soil	Thin infertile soil
Resources	Coal, minerals, timber	Few natural resources
Access	Coastal areas	Inland areas
Economy	Plenty of industry and jobs	Lack of industry and jobs

Birth and death rates

- World population growth is caused by birth rates being greater than death rates.
- **Birth rate** = the number of births per 1 000 people per year.
- **Death rate** = the number of deaths per 1 000 people per year.

natural increase

population increases because the birth rate is higher than the death rate

natural decrease

population decreases because the death rate is higher than the birth rate

World population growth

- For most of human history the world's population remained steady. It took until 1800 for it to reach one billion; today the world's population is over six billion.
- This rapid growth in world population is called the **population explosion** and was the result of reduced death rates due to improvements in medicine.

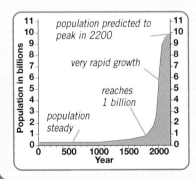

- Global population growth is now beginning to slow – it is predicted the population will stabilise at 10.4 billion people in 2200.
- Population growth is not spread equally between countries – 95% of growth is in LEDCs.
- MEDCs have reached a replacement level of population growth or are experiencing a decrease.

KEY TERMS

Make sure you understand these terms before moving on!
- birth rate
- death rate
- densely populated
- population
- population density
- population distribution
- population explosion
- sparsely populated

QUICK TEST

1. What is the difference between population distribution and population density?
2. Is India densely or sparsely populated?
3. What is the population explosion?
4. What would happen to a country's population if the death rate was higher than the birth rate?

Population change

Graphs can be used to show the make-up of populations and how populations change over time. Governments may try to control the way their country's population grows.

Demographic transition model

n The **demographic transition model** shows how changes in birth rates and death rates have affected global population growth.

n The model may be used to explain population change in four stages (see diagram).

n MEDCs are entering a fifth stage where death rates exceed birth rates and populations are falling.

stage 1
- *birth rates high Ë no birth control, children needed for labour*
- *death rates high Ë poor hygiene and disease*
- *population growth = very slow*

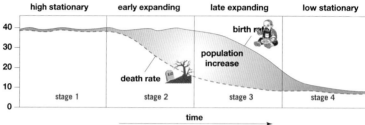

high stationary | early expanding | late expanding | low stationary

births and deaths per thousand per year — 40 30 20 10 0

birth rate

population increase

death rate

stage 1 | stage 2 | stage 3 | stage 4

time

stage 4
- *birth rates low Ë contraception, low infant mortality*
- *death rates low Ë high quality health care*
- *population growth = steady, fluctuating*

stage 2
- *birth rates still high*
- *death rates fall Ë improved sanitation, healthcare and diet*
- *population growth = rapid*

stage 3
- *birth rates fall Ë birth control, increased wealth, women's rights*
- *death rates fall slowly*
- *population growth = slow*

Population control

Before trying to reduce global population growth it is vital to understand the reasons why people in LEDCs have large families:

n Labour – children are needed to work to provide income.

n Old age – people without pensions rely on their children to support them.

n Infant mortality – poor health care means not all children survive to adulthood.

n Religion – Catholicism and Islam disapprove of birth control.

n Contraception – birth control methods may not be available.

Some MEDCs with falling populations are trying to encourage population growth. France gives generous child benefit and maternity leave to try to persuade people to have more children.

Governments may encourage people to have fewer children through:

n Advertising – attempting to change attitudes and culture.

n Financial – offering bonuses to those with small families.

n Education – teaching women about family planning.

n Healthcare – reducing the infant mortality rate and providing contraception.

n Law – rules limiting the number of children.

Case study: population control

Location: China
Population: 1.3 billion

Population policy

■ 1979 – one child per family policy announced.
■ Permission is necessary to marry and have children.
■ Women must be at least 25 to marry.
■ Free health care, monthly allowance and improved pension for one-child families.
■ Fines for parents having two children.

■ Forced abortions and sterilisations have been reported.

Effects of policy

■ Birth rates have fallen and population growth has slowed.
■ Boys are more valued than girls ➡ female babies have been abandoned.
■ Population is becoming unbalanced ➡ 110 males to 100 females.
■ Ageing population will cause dependency problems.

The one child policy has been relaxed in recent years. Women may be allowed to have a second child if the first is a girl.

Population structure

■ **Population structure** is the make-up of a population in terms of age, sex and **life expectancy**.
■ Population structures are shown as a **population pyramid**.

Population pyramids

■ Population is divided into 5-year age groups.
■ Horizontal bars show the percentage of the population in each age group.

narrow peak – short life expectancy

males age females

LEDC pyramid
(stage 1)
e.g. India

steep, concave sides – high infant mortality rate and death rate

80+
75–79
70–74
65–69
60–64
55–60
50–54
45–49
40–44
35–39
30–34
25–29
20–25
15–19
10–14
5–9
0–4

10   5   0   0   5   10
% of total population

wide base – high birth rate ➡ and large percentage of children

wider peak – long life expectancy

males age females

MEDC pyramid
(stage 4)
e.g. UK

vertical sides – low infant mortality rate and death rate

90+
85–89
80–84
75–79
70–74
65–69
60–64
55–60
50–54
45–49
40–44
35–39
30–34
25–29
20–25
15–19
10–14
5–9
0–4

5 4 3 2 1 0   0 1 2 3 4 5
% of total population

narrowing base – low and falling birth rate ➡ low percentage of children

■ Males are shown on the left; females on the right.
■ Trends in birth rates, death rates, infant mortality rates and life expectancy can be identified.
■ LEDCs and MEDCs have different shaped pyramids.

KEY TERMS

Make sure you understand these terms before moving on!
■ demographic transition model
■ life expectancy
■ population control
■ population pyramid
■ population structure

QUICK TEST

1 Why does rapid population growth occur in stage two of the demographic transition model?

2 At what stage of the demographic transition model is the UK?

3 What age are the 'economically active' in a population?

4 How is the Chinese population becoming unbalanced?

5 What is meant by the term population structure?

Migration

Migration is the movement of people from one place to another.

Push factors are things about the origin that encourage, or force, people to leave.

Pull factors are things about the destination that attract people.

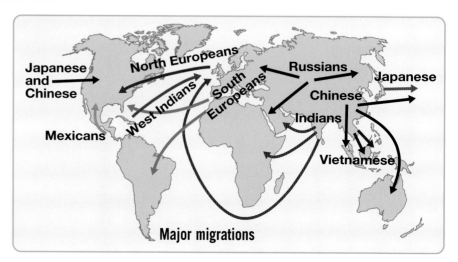

Major migrations

Types of migration

Migration can be classified into different categories.
- **Immigration** is the movement of people into a country.
- **Emigration** is the movement of people out of a country.

International migration is controlled by governments. They may encourage or discourage migration into their country. Illegal migrants will be returned to their country of origin (deported).

Internal – same country	International – between countries
Permanent – stay for good	Temporary – return home later
Voluntary – own choice	Forced – no choice

 INTERNET
Refugees and migration
http://www.oneworld.org/guides/
migration/index.html

Rural to urban migration

- **Rural to urban migration** is the movement of people from the countryside to cities. This process is called urbanisation. Today urbanisation is happening mainly in LEDCs.
- **Push factors** – few jobs, poor wages, poor health care and few education opportunities.
- **Pull factors** – formal and informal jobs, higher wages, clinics, more schools and excitement of city life.

Impacts
- City – life for migrants is tough, jobs are hard to find, services are over-stretched, many live in squatter settlements.
- Countryside – becomes depopulated ➡ fewer farmers so food production declines, unbalanced population structure dominated by women, children, sick and older people.

Urban to rural migration

- **Urban to rural migration** is the movement of people from cities back to the countryside. This process is called counter-urbanisation. Counter-urbanisation is happening mainly in MEDCs.
- Push factors – lack of open space, noise, air pollution, traffic congestion, fear of crime.
- Pull factors – attractive countryside, safer for children, larger houses, improved transport makes commuting possible.

Impacts
- Inner city – becomes depopulated ➡ housing empty and boarded up ➡ services decline.
- Countryside – under pressure for new housing developments ➡ friction between locals and newcomers.

International migration

- International migration is the movement of people from one country to another.
- Most international migrants are moving for economic or social reasons. They are seeking a better standard of living, or wish to be with relatives.

Case Study: USA and Mexico situation

- 2 000 km border between USA and Mexico.
- 1 million + Mexicans migrate to USA each year.
- Illegal migration is a problem for USA and Mexico.
- US Border Patrol guard border against illegal migrants.

Push and pull factors

- The USA needs seasonal workers for farms and food-processing factories.
- Wages are much higher in the USA ➡ workers can earn 10 times more than in Mexico.
- Education in the USA is free for children of legal, and illegal, migrants.
- Quality of life is lower in Mexico.

Impacts

- Mexican migrants benefit the US economy by working for low wages.

- Mexican culture has enriched the US border states – food, music, language.
- Illegal migration costs USA millions of dollars – Border Patrol, prisons.
- Mexican countryside has a shortage of economically active people.

Refugees

- **Refugees** are people who have been forced to leave their home country because of war, persecution or natural disasters.
- The United Nations estimate there are over 13 million refugees spread throughout 140 countries.

Case Study: Rwanda Situation

- Rwanda is a small country in Central Africa.
- Population divided into two ethnic groups – Hutu and Tutsi.
- In 1994 over 2 million Hutus fled Rwanda and became refugees.

Push and pull factors

- Tension between the Hutu and Tutsi ethnic groups.
- April 1994 – Hutu people began massacre of 800 000 Tutsis.
- July 1994 – Tutsis formed army and began to fight back.
- Hutus fled to safety in neighbouring countries.

Impacts

- Refugee camps set up in Zaire, Tanzania and Burundi.
- Lack of food and clean water ➡ 50 000 Hutus died in a week.
- Overcrowding in camps ➡ crime and violence.
- Environmental damage ➡ deforestation for firewood and shelters.

KEY TERMS

- emigration
- immigration
- migration
- pull factors
- push factors
- refugees
- rural to urban migration
- urban to rural migration

QUICK TEST

1. What is emigration?
2. What is urbanisation?
3. What is counter-urbanisation?
4. What are the main reasons for international migration?
5. Why do people become refugees?

Settlement

■ Settlement began 10 000 years ago when nomadic people learned to cultivate crops.

■ A settlement is a place where people live, ranging from a single house to a city.

The *functions* of a settlement are its social and economic activities:

■ **Residential** – providing places for people to live.

■ **Administrative** – local authority offices.

■ Functions may change over time

■ **Industrial** – factories and business parks.

■ **Commercial** – shopping centres and recreational facilities.

■ **Services** – public services such as schools, hospitals and libraries.

Site and situation

- **Site** is the exact location of a settlement.
- Today many of the reasons for the location of settlements are outdated.
- **Situation** is the location of a settlement in relation to the surrounding area. A settlement with good access to natural resources and to other settlements will grow in size.

Relief – high enough to be safe from flooding, low enough to be sheltered from wind.

Defence – hilltop or inside of river meander provides protection from attackers.

Water supply – clean water needed for drinking, cooking and cleaning.

Fuel – wood needed to burn for cooking and heat.

Transport – site on a crossroads, river or the coast made access to other places easier.

hills

river

wood

quarry

flat land

cross roads

deep fertile soil

Soil – deep fertile soil made farming easier.   Resources – timber or rock needed for building.

Case study : Paris – site and situation

Paris – capital of France
Population – 10 million
Established – third century BC

SITUATION
Paris is a focus of roads throughout France and Europe.

International airports provide global links.

Paris is a centre of European rail networks.

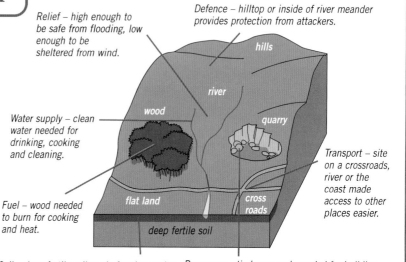

R. Oise

A15

A1

R. Seine

A13

original site of Paris

Paris
Airport
Forest
Farmland

A10

A4

A6

R. Seine

SITE
Settlement first began on small island in River Seine.

Site was good for defence and also as a key river crossing point.

River Seine provided water supply.

Fertile soil of River Seine's floodplain was excellent for farming.

Forest provided fuel and building materials.

Settlement hierarchy

- Settlements may be arranged in rank order – a **hierarchy**. These can be shown using a pyramid. The order of importance is decided using three criteria:
  - population size
  - services (range and number)
  - distance apart from other similar settlements.
- A mega-city is at the top of the hierarchy because it has a high population, a large range and number of services, and will be a long distance from other mega-cities.
- A hamlet is at the bottom of the hierarchy because it has only a few people living there, possibly no services, and it is likely to be close to other hamlets.

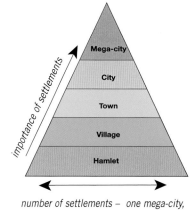

number of settlements – one mega-city, thousands of hamlets

A mega-city is a city with a population of over 10 million.

Sphere of influence

- The **sphere of influence** is the area served by a settlement – also called a catchment area.
- Sphere of influence is determined by the range and threshold of services.

Range

- Range is the maximum distance people are prepared to travel to use a service.
- Goods bought frequently are called convenience goods ➡ weekly shopping ➡ people only travel short distances.
- Goods bought infrequently are called comparison goods ➡ furniture ➡ people travel greater distances.

Threshold

- Threshold is the minimum number of people needed to support a service.
- Shops selling convenience goods have low threshold populations.
- Shops selling comparison goods have high threshold populations.

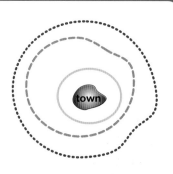

———— newsagent
– – – – cinema
········ hospital

The larger the settlement, the greater the number of services, and the wider its sphere of influence.

KEY TERMS

Make sure you understand these terms before moving on!

- functions
- hierarchy
- range
- site
- situation
- sphere of influence
- threshold

QUICK TEST

1. What is the difference between site and situation?
2. What is meant by settlement function?
3. What type of settlement is at the top of a settlement hierarchy?
4. What term describes the maximum distance people are prepared to travel to use a service?
5. Which will have a larger threshold – a newsagent or a supermarket?

Settlement in MEDCs

■ **Urban areas in MEDCs expanded during the Industrial Revolution.**

Urbanisation

- **Urbanisation** in MEDCs increased significantly as a result of the Industrial Revolution during the nineteenth century.
- People migrated from the countryside to towns looking for work in factories.
- Terraced houses were built to accommodate workers.
- Over time, towns expanded to become cities.
- During the twentieth century, shops and offices replaced factories in the city centre to form a **Central Business District** (CBD).

Urbanisation is an increase in the percentage of people living in cities – **urban growth** is the expansion of cities into the surrounding countryside.

Urban problems
- Inner-city areas had become very run-down by the 1960s and 1970s.
- Factories had closed down due to poor access, outdated technology and competition from factories in better locations.
- Unemployment grew, neighbourhoods declined and better-off people moved to the suburbs.
- Inner-city housing was old, cramped, often damp and unhealthy.
- Public transport systems were struggling to cope and traffic congestion was becoming worse.

Case study: urban redevelopment – London Docklands

The London Docklands used to be the busiest docks in the world. By the 1980s ships had become too large to sail up the Thames, and competition from elsewhere forced the docks to close, with the loss of 13 000 jobs.

The London Docklands Development Corporation (LDDC) was formed to redevelop the area. Between 1981 and 1998 they spent £10 billion improving this part of east London.

Impacts

Urban regeneration – disused docks redeveloped with a mixture of housing, offices and shops, for example, Canary Wharf.

Housing development – derelict land was cleared to build 24 000 new homes, ranging from local authority housing to luxury apartment blocks.

Transport – accessibility has been improved with the addition of the Docklands Light Railway,

Jubilee Underground extension, London City Airport and 90km of new roads.

Gentrification – warehouses next to the docks have been converted into very expensive luxury apartments, and 130 hectares of parkland have been created.

Cultural venues such as the Docklands Arena and Millennium Dome have been built, and the area will play a key role in the 2012 Olympics.

Twenty-first century urban issues

The UK government has predicted that over 4 million new homes will be needed in England by 2016. More homes are needed because of changes in lifestyle.

- People are living longer
- More marriages are ending in divorce
- People want to live in the countryside

Options for new housing
Greenfield sites

- **Greenfield sites** are rural locations that have not been built on before.
- Greenfield sites are popular with developers as they are easier and cheaper to build on.

- Building on greenfield sites can lead to urban sprawl as cities continue to expand.
- Greenfield housing developments encourage further building – business parks, retail parks and leisure facilities.

Brownfield sites

- **Brownfield sites** are areas of wasteland in towns and cities.
- The government target is to build 60% of new homes on brownfield sites.
- Brownfield sites are expensive to build on because they are often contaminated with industrial waste.

- In England there are over one million empty buildings that could be converted into new homes.

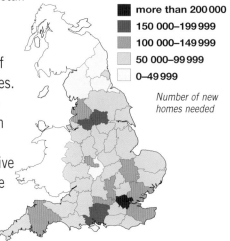

| more than 200 000 |
| 150 000–199 999 |
| 100 000–149 999 |
| 50 000–99 999 |
| 0–49 999 |

Number of new homes needed

Urban land use model

- As urban areas grow they develop zones of different land uses.
- Models, such as Burgess' **concentric circle model** have been created to try to explain the different land-use zones in cities.

Concentric circle model (Burgess)

- Central Business District (CBD) of shops and offices is at the centre.
- Transition zone surrounds the CBD – old housing, abandoned industry and derelict land is being redeveloped.
- Low-cost housing – old terraced housing and blocks of flats.
- Medium-cost housing – renovated terraced houses and older semi-detached houses.
- High-cost housing – modern estates of semi-detached and detached houses on the city outskirts (suburbs).

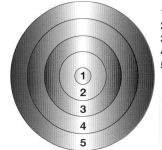

1 CBD
2 transition zone
3 low-cost housing
4 medium-cost housing
5 high-cost housing

The inner city, in the transition zone, is an area at or near the city centre with dilapidated housing, derelict land and declining industry.

 You should be able to compare this land use model with a settlement you have studied.

KEY TERMS

Make sure you understand these terms before moving on!

- brownfield sites
- central Business District
- concentric circle model
- greenfield sites
- urban growth
- urbanisation

QUICK TEST

1. What triggered urbanisation in MEDCs?
2. What is the CBD?
3. What is the difference between urbanisation and urban growth?
4. What is the inner city?
5. Why do houses become bigger towards the suburbs?

Settlement in LEDCs

In 1950 there were 80 cities in the world with populations of over one million. Today there are over 300 'million cities' world wide. This growth has been dominated by rapid urbanisation in LEDCs.

City	Urban population (millions)	City	Urban population (millions)
Tokyo, Japan	34.9	Delhi, India	14.1
Mexico City, Mexico	18.6	Kolkata, India	13.8
New York, USA	18.2	Buenos Aires, Argentina	13.0
Sao Paolo, Brazil	17.8	Shanghai, China	12.7
Mumbai, India	17.4	Jakarta, Indonesia	12.2

Urbanisation

Urbanisation in LEDCs began later than in MEDCs, and under different circumstances.

Rural to urban migration
- **Rural to urban migration** has increased the relative proportion of people living in cities.
- Poor harvests, lack of money and inadequate services have 'pushed' people from the countryside.
- Possibility of paid employment, better education and health care have 'pulled' people to cities.

Population growth
- **Population growth** is generally higher in LEDCs than in MEDCs and this has also led to an increase in urban populations.
- Population growth remains high because people continue to have large families at the same time as improved health care is reducing death rates.

Approximately 30% of people in LEDCs now live in urban areas. This figure is lower than in MEDCs, but urbanisation in LEDCs is happening extremely quickly.

Urban land use model

LEDC cities have developed different land use zones compared to MEDC cities.

- **Central Business District** (CBD) of shops and offices – looks very similar to MEDC cities.
- High-quality housing – expensive apartments and large houses on best-quality land, close to CBD and along main roads.

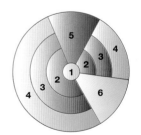

1 CBD
2 medium-cost housing
3 low-cost housing
4 shanty towns
5 high-cost housing
6 industry

- Medium-quality housing – oldest housing, improved by occupants over several decades.
- Low-quality housing – self-built using breeze blocks and corrugated iron (improved shanty towns).
- **Shanty towns** – newest housing on the city outskirts built from scrap, wood, metal and plastic.
- Industry – zones of industry have developed along roads and railways.
- In general, the quality of housing decreases as distance from the CBD increases.

Case study : Jakarta, Indonesia

- Jakarta, the capital city of Indonesia, has grown rapidly since the 1950s.
- It is now the largest city in South-East Asia – population 14 million.
- Growth of Jakarta is mainly a result of rural – urban migration caused by a shortage of land in the countryside, and the possibility of paid work in the city.
- As an LEDC city, Jakarta contains everything from shiny new apartment blocks to squalid shanty towns.

Problems

- Unemployment and poverty – large numbers of migrants to Jakarta are unable to find regular jobs. The jobs that are available are often low paid and dangerous.
- Housing – shortage of cheap housing means many migrants live in appalling conditions in Jakarta's shanty towns.
- Services – basic services are in short supply. Many people have no running water and must pump water by hand. There is no mains sewage system so human waste is removed by special lorries, if at all.
- Traffic – congestion is becoming worse as the number of cars, lorries and autotaxis increase.

Solutions

- Transnational companies have been encouraged to provide jobs.
- New towns have been built on the city outskirts to provide more housing.
- Shanty towns have been destroyed and apartment blocks built in their place.
- Self-help schemes have helped the poorest people to build their own homes.
- Water supplies are being improved.
- Road congestion is being tackled by building large flyovers throughout the city.
- Railway network is being improved.

INTERNET

Cities of today, cities of tomorrow

http://www.un.org/Pubs/CyberSchoolBus/special/habitat/index.html

---

KEY TERMS

Make sure you understand these terms before moving on!
- central business district
- population growth
- rural to urban migration
- shanty towns
- urban land use model
- urbanisation

QUICK TEST

1. What is a million city?
2. What two factors are causing rapid urbanisation in LEDCs?
3. What is a shanty town?
4. Whereabouts are shanty towns found in LEDC cities?
5. What steps have the Indonesian government taken to provide more jobs in Jakarta?

Agriculture

Agriculture is the growing of crops and rearing of animals. Agriculture provides the world's population with food and other essential products.

Farming as a system

Farming works as a system with inputs, processes and outputs.

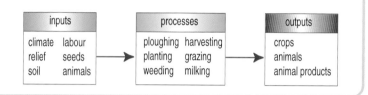

inputs		processes		outputs
climate	labour	ploughing	harvesting	crops
relief	seeds	planting	grazing	animals
soil	animals	weeding	milking	animal products

Classification

Agriculture may be classified into a range of different types:

- **Arable** – growing of crops such as wheat or barley.
- **Pastoral** – rearing of animals for meat and other animal products.
- Mixed – a combination of arable and pastoral farming.
- Intensive – relatively high input of money, labour or technology over a small area to produce high yields per hectare.

- Extensive – relatively low input of money, labour or technology over a large area to produce low yields per hectare.
- Commercial – produces food for sale and profit.
- Subsistence – produces food for the farmer's family; small surpluses may be sold.
- Nomadic – shifting cultivation or seasonal movements of livestock for pasture.
- Sedentary – farming in a fixed location.

Factors affecting farming

Physical factors
- Rainfall – crops need between 250 mm and 500 mm of regular rainfall per year.
- Temperature – crops need a minimum temperature of 6°C to grow.
- Growing season – length of time crops need to grow; for example wheat needs 90 days.
- Altitude – temperatures decrease on average by 6°C every 1000 metres.
- Aspect – south-facing slopes receive most sunshine.
- Relief – steep slopes result in thin soils and limit use of machinery.
- Soil – deep, fertile, well-drained soils are best for crops.

Human factors
- Labour – farming requires either human labour or mechanisation.
- Market – demand for agricultural products – markets are now global.
- Accessibility – transport costs increase with distance from market.
- Subsidies – governments provide money to encourage some types of farming.
- Quotas – governments place limits on production to prevent surpluses.
- Attitudes – personal interests will also influence farmers' decisions.

Farming in the UK

Dairy farming
- Rearing of cattle for milk and meat products.
- Locations: Western parts of England, Scotland and Wales.
- Physical factors: flat land, fertile well-drained soils, high-quality grass, mild winters and reliable rainfall.
- Human factors: rapid access to large urban markets, subsidies for milk production after 1945 and milk quotas introduced in the 1980s.

Market gardening
- Intensive farming of high-value crops such as fruit and salad vegetables.
- Locations: South-East England, Fens, Isles of Scilly.
- Physical factors: hours of sunshine, most other physical factors are controlled in glasshouses.
- Human factors: high inputs of capital, consumer tastes and access to markets. Produce is transported by refrigerated lorries and aeroplanes.

Sheep and beef cattle farming
- Cattle reared for meat; sheep for meat and wool.
- Locations: upland areas in England, Wales and Scotland.
- Physical factors: high, steep land, thin infertile soils, high rainfall and low temperatures.
- Human factors: cattle and beef are the most economic types of farming, subsidies are provided by the EU.

Arable Farming
- Growing of cereal crops, vegetables and animal feeds.
- Locations: East and South-East England, East Scotland.
- Physical factors: flat land, deep rich soils, relatively dry climate, reliable rain in growing season, warm summers and frost in winter to break up soil.
- Human factors: minimum prices for arable products guaranteed by EU (price support).

arable
mixed
dairy cattle
sheep and beef cattle
market gardening

INTERNET
National Farmer's Union
http://www.nfu.org.uk/education/default.asp

KEY TERMS
Make sure you understand these terms before moving on!
- arable
- arable farming
- dairy farming
- human factors
- market gardening
- pastoral
- physical factors
- sheep and beef cattle farming

QUICK TEST
1. Classify the following as farming inputs, processes or outputs: crops, harvesting, profit, soil, grazing, climate
2. How does altitude affect farming?
3. What is a quota?
4. What is the difference between subsistence and commercial farming?
5. Where are the main locations of arable farming in the UK?

Agricultural change

A rapidly increasing global population is causing a rising demand for food. Changes in agriculture have brought benefits and problems in both MEDCs and LEDCs.

Changes in MEDCs

Set Aside
- **Set aside** is an EU-funded scheme intended to reduce surpluses.
- Farmers are paid not to cultivate up to 20% of their land for five years.
- Land may be left fallow, planted with trees or used for non-agricultural purposes.

Diversification
- **Diversification** is when farmers develop business initiatives other than farming.
- Barns are converted into holiday cottages.
- Garden centres and farm shops sell local produce.
- Tea shops with children's play areas and petting zoos.

Organic farming
- Public demand for **organic** produce has increased following food scares such as BSE in cattle, and trials of Genetically Modified crops.
- Crops are grown without artificial chemical fertilisers.
- Animals are reared without using drugs and chemicals.

Environmental impacts of farming in MEDCs

Modern intensive farming techniques have had an impact on the environment.

Hedgerow removal
- Hedgerows have been removed to make fields bigger and improve access for large farm machinery.
- 377 000 km of hedgerows have been removed since 1945 in the UK.
- Wildlife has declined due to loss of habitats.

Nitrate pollution
- Overuse of fertiliser leads to **nitrate pollution** rivers and lakes.

nitrates sprayed on fields

nitrates cause algae to grow and use up oxygen

nitrates washed over surface

nitrates collect in rivers and lakes

algae

roots absorb nitrates

dead fish due to lack of oxygen

nitrates flow through soil

Common Agricultural Policy

Common Agricultural Policy (CAP) – agreed by UK and other European countries (European Union) in 1962. It has three aims:
- To protect farmers' incomes.
- To ensure reasonable and steady prices.
- To increase production.

The CAP achieves these aims through two main policies:
- Grants and subsidies – money provided for farmers in difficult areas, such as hill farms.
- Price support – a guaranteed minimum price for agricultural produce ➡ bought and stored by the EU ➡ sold when prices are high enough ➡ may cause large surpluses.

The CAP is very expensive taking up 40% of the budget of the EU. As a result the EU is trying to reduce the amount of money paid to farmers.

Changes in LEDCs

- Population growth in LEDCs has led to an increased demand for food production.
- High-technology farming methods were introduced in the 1960s and 1970s.
- Food production rose dramatically, but with some problems.
- Today, appropriate technology farming methods are considered more appropriate for many poorer countries.

Green Revolution

- The **Green Revolution** was the introduction of capital-intensive farming methods in LEDCs.
- **High Yield Variety crops** – HYV crops of rice and wheat are faster growing and more hardy therefore produce an increase in yield.
- Fertilisers – artificial fertilisers are used to feed HYV crops.
- Herbicides and pesticides – weeds and pests are controlled with chemicals.
- Irrigation – HYV crops require more water than traditional varieties.
- Machinery – farm processes mechanised ➡ buffalo replaced by tractors.

    The Green Revolution was concentrated in Asia and South America.

Successes

- Yields have increased by up to three times.
- Quick-growing HYV plants allow two crops per year.
- Countries now export grain rather than import it.

Problems

- Poorer farmers could not afford HYV crops.
- HYV crops need more expensive fertilisers and pesticides.
- Mechanisation increased rural unemployment.
- Monoculture (one breed of crop) carries a greater risk of disease destroying entire crop.
- Much of the increase in production is exported – poor cannot afford to buy it.

Appropriate technology

- Water supply – wells, pumps and drip irrigation provide a cheap and effective means of providing water for crops.
- Soil erosion – trees are planted as windbreaks to prevent soil being blown away; stone lines are built along contours to stop soil being washed away by rain.
- Soil fertility – leguminous crops fix nitrogen in the soil, increasing soil fertility.
- Inter-cropping – crops may be grown at different heights to maximise productivity – trees, plants and root vegetables.
- Food storage – well-designed grain stores prevent losses from rats, insects and disease.

Make sure you understand these terms before moving on!

- Common Agricultural Policy (CAP)
- diversification
- Green Revolution
- High Yield Variety crops
- nitrate pollution
- organic
- Set Aside

QUICK TEST

1. What is 'farm diversification'?
2. How does nitrate pollution harm the environment?
3. Why has the amount of hedgerows in the UK decreased?
4. What was the Green Revolution?
5. Why did poorer farmers not benefit from the Green Revolution?

Agriculture case studies

Hill Farming, Wales, UK

(Hill farming, commercial, extensive)

Location
- Merthyr Farm, Harlech, Snowdonia, Wales
- A 140 hectare hill farm rearing sheep for meat and wool, and cattle for meat

Physical factors
- Relief: steep hills ranging from 180 and 360 metres above sea level.
- Soil: light soil, shallow and stony, naturally deficient in nutrients. Lower slopes can become waterlogged.
- Climate: precipitation 1250mm to 1500mm per year, average winter temperature 5°C, average summer temperature 15°C.

Human factors
- The harsh environment means that the farm is classified as a Less Favoured Area and therefore receives half of its income as EU subsidies and grants.
- Payments are also made to the farm for its conservation of dry stone walls.

Farm system

Inputs	Processes	Outputs
3 full time and 3 part time workers Fertiliser to improve grazing areas Pesticides to control bracken Stock feed e.g. beet and straw Diesel for machinery	Lambing Calving Field spraying Shearing Silage making Farm tours Dry stone walling	750 lambs 110 ewes 18 bullocks 1200kg wool 650 bales of silage

Recent problems and changes
- The BSE crisis reduced the price of cattle, though no animals were directly affected.
- The price of lamb is falling, and EU subsidies are under threat. Wool prices are very low and farmers have to pay the shearers more than the fleeces are worth. Some hill farmers are giving up, or emigrating.
- The farm has recently been registered to sell "Farm Assured" stock. Vets inspect the farm. They look at a wide variety of features including feed storage, handling facilities, the medicine store, farm records and animal welfare.

Market Gardening, Netherlands, EU

(Market gardening, commercial, intensive)

Location
- Van den Berg farm, Breezand, northern Holland
- 52 hectare tulip and daffodil bulb growing farm

Physical factors
- Relief: flat, land just above sea level behind coastal sand dunes. Dunes provide shelter from coastal winds.
- Soil: sandy soil, well drained and lime rich
- Climate: precipitation 830mm per year, evenly distributed, average winter temperature 3°C, average summer temperature 17°C.

Human factors
- Land is expensive and therefore high value crops are essential.
- The farm is a family business that has been handed down over four generations
- The farm is part of a co-operative that helps share the cost or trialing new bulb varieties.
- Government funded scientific research and advisory services support Dutch bulb growers.

 INTERNET
Farming and Countryside Education
http://www.face-online.org.uk

Farm system

Inputs	Processes	Outputs
6 full time workers Many seasonal workers Fertiliser for fields Pesticides to control insects Herbicides to control weeds Energy for drying bulbs	Planting Irrigation Field spraying Flower head cutting Bulb harvesting Bulb drying and packing	Total of 2 million bulbs 12 varieties of tulips Daffodils Lilies Speciality bulbs

Rice Farming, Philippines, LEDC

(Rice farming, subsistence, intensive)

Location
- Sitio Batol Farm, Luzon, Philippines
- A 0.5 hectare rice farm

Physical factors
- Relief: flat coastal land reaching 60m above sea level.
- Soil: fertile clay
- Climate: monsoon climate with 2000mm of precipitation per year, but 80% falls between June and October, average temperature 25°C.

Human factors
- Land is expensive and therefore high value crops are essential.
- The farm is too small to provide enough money and therefore the farmer's wife works abroad providing 80% of the family income.
- The farmers do not own the land they farm, and have to pay rent to the landowner.

Farm system

Inputs	Processes	Outputs
4 full time workers 4 children help when needed Fertiliser for rice (paddy) fields Pesticides to control snails Stock feed for 2 cattle	Rice planting Weeding Field spraying Rice harvesting Grass cutting for cows	3150 kg of rice for home consumption 450 kg of rice to landowner 400 kg of rice for rent of machinery One calf sold per year

KEY TERMS

Make sure you understand these terms before moving on!
- hill farming
- market gardening
- rice farming

QUICK TEST

1. Name an example of an extensive, commercial farm.
2. Name an example of an intensive, subsistence farm.
3. What is the benefit of farming in a Less Favoured Area?
4. Why is it necessary to grow high value crops in the Netherlands?

Industry

■ *Industry* is any type of economic activity, or employment, producing goods or providing services.

Classification

Industry is divided into four types:

primary	secondary	tertiary	quaternary

1. **Primary** industry extraction or production of raw materials – includes agriculture, forestry, fishing and mining.

2. **Secondary** industry processing of raw materials, or assembling components to manufacture a finished product – includes steel-making and car assembly.

3. **Tertiary** industry services such as health, administration, retailing and transport – also called 'service industries'.

4. **Quaternary** industry providing advice or information, or research and development – includes work in biotechnology, communications and information technology.

Industry as a system

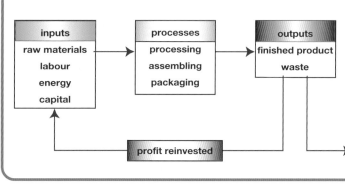

■ Industry operates as a system with inputs, processes and outputs.
■ Finished product is sold and money earned is re-invested in the industry to buy more raw materials, pay wages, bills and repay loans.
■ Profit is the money left after re-investment
  ➡ paid to shareholders in a large company.

Occupational structures

■ **Occupational structures** (employment structures) describe the percentage of workers involved in primary, secondary and tertiary industry in an area.
■ Occupational structures are shown as a pie chart.
■ Occupational structures change over time as a country experiences industrialisation and de-industrialisation.
■ Industrialisation is the development of a manufacturing-based society, having been dependent on agriculture.
■ De-industrialisation is the move away from manufacturing to a society based on service industries.
■ LEDCs have a high percentage of workers in primary industry.
■ MEDCs have the majority of workers employed in tertiary industry.

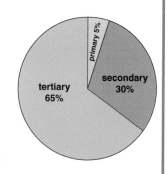

Location of industry

The location of industry is influenced by a large number of factors:

- Raw materials – distance from raw materials affects transport costs
- Market – access to people who will purchase the goods or services
- Labour – employees with different skills are needed
- Energy – most industries use electricity, some heavy industries require coal
- Site – modern factories require large areas of flat land, especially if using an assembly line
- Transport – road, rail, sea and air transport networks are required for the import and export of goods communications – reliable telecommunications are increasingly important
- Capital – money needed to set up the industry
- Government policy – industry is restricted in some areas and encouraged in others with the use of grants, rent-free buildings and low taxes
- Environment – an attractive environment with good leisure facilities may be important to attract workers.

Industrial inertia – industries may remain in an area although it may no longer be the most economic location.

Industrial linkages

- Industries are linked to other industries because they supply each other with products and services.
- This means many small industries may be dependent on the success of a larger industry.
- Industrial linkages result in the **multiplier effect**. The multiplier effect works in reverse if a large industry closes down.

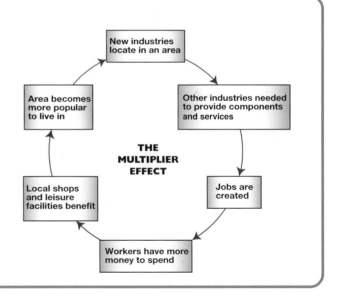

New industries locate in an area

Other industries needed to provide components and services

THE MULTIPLIER EFFECT

Jobs are created

Workers have more money to spend

Local shops and leisure facilities benefit

Area becomes more popular to live in

KEY TERMS

Make sure you understand these terms before moving on!
- industry
- occupational structures
- primary
- quaternary
- secondary
- tertiary
- multiplier effect

QUICK TEST

❶ Classify the following jobs as primary, secondary, tertiary or quaternary: teacher, miner, software developer, baker.

❷ What is industrial inertia?

❸ Classify the following as industrial inputs, processes or outputs: packaging, labour, energy, finished product, assembling, waste.

❹ Describe the employment structure shown by the pie chart under the "Occupational Structures" heading on p.68.

❺ Does the pie chart show an MEDC or an LEDC?

Industry in MEDCs

Location of heavy industry

- **Heavy industry** developed in the UK during the **Industrial Revolution** of the nineteenth century.
- Invention of mechanisation using steam power led to an enormous increase in manufacturing.
- The most important industries were coal mining, iron and steel manufacturing and textile milling.
- Factories and mills were built close to raw materials.
- Thousands of workers migrated from the countryside in search of jobs ➡ industrial towns and cities expanded.

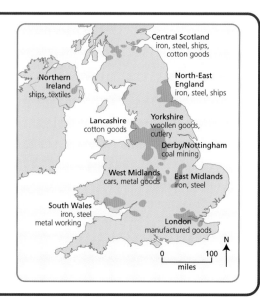

Deindustrialisation

By the 1960s heavy industry in the UK was in serious decline for two main reasons:

Labour costs
- Standards of living had risen in the UK, and so had wages.
- Lower wages in other countries meant goods could be produced much more cheaply abroad.
- Competition from abroad made the UK's heavy industries uneconomic.

World market
- Raw materials such as coal and iron ore were being mined much more cheaply in huge open-cast mines in countries such as Australia and the USA.
- Most of the UK's colonies had gained independence. They were now free to import goods from whichever **market** they chose – not just the UK.

Case study : iron and steel industry – South Wales

During the nineteenth century, South Wales became the most important metal-producing area in the world. Today, only two steel factories remain.

Key location factors
- **Raw materials** – coal and iron ore from valleys, limestone from Brecon Beacons.
- Markets – British colonies such as India and Australia.
- **Labour** – 500 000 people migrated from rural areas.

Decline
- Raw materials – iron ore deposits used up, coal seams too narrow for modern mining.
- Markets – ex-colonies have developed their own steel industries, global demand for steel has fallen.
- Labour – thousands of coal miners and steel workers made redundant due to closure of mines and steel plants.
- Environment – 200 years of industry have severely polluted the land.

Modern industry

Modern industries have taken over from heavy industries in MEDCs:

- Light manufacturing – small products, e.g. electrical goods, food processing.
- High-tech industry – high-value products, e.g. computers, mobile phones.
- Retail industry – shops and out-of-town shopping centres.
- Leisure industry – cinemas, restaurants, sports centres.
- Administration – offices and telephone call centres.

Case study – Auto Europa

Company – Ford / Volkswagen AutoEuropa car plant
Location – Setubal, Portugal
Business – assembling Multi-Purpose Vehicles (MPV)

Key location factors

- Transport – new docks built in Setubal to export cars on specially designed car-transporter ships, and a new road link with Lisbon via the 10 mile long Vasco da Gama bridge.

- Labour – large workforce available with wages in Portugal much lower than in north European countries. The factory directly employs 3000 people.

Location of modern industries

- Modern industries are described as **footloose**. They do not use heavy or bulky raw materials so are able to locate wherever they choose.
- The two most important factors affecting location are transport and labour.
- Modern industries prefer to locate on greenfield sites – locations on the edge of urban areas which have not been built on before:
  - Industrial estates – light manufacturing companies.
  - Business parks – mixture of light manufacturing, offices and retail.
  - Science parks – high-tech companies linked to a university.
  - Retail parks – mixture of large shops and leisure facilities.

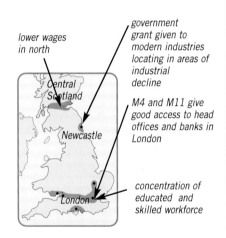

government grant given to modern industries locating in areas of industrial decline

M4 and M11 give good access to head offices and banks in London

concentration of educated and skilled workforce

lower wages in north

Central Scotland

Newcastle

London

KEY TERMS

Make sure you understand these terms before moving on!
- footloose
- industrial revolution
- labour
- market
- modern industries
- raw materials

QUICK TEST

❶ What invention led to the Industrial Revolution?

❷ Which raw material powered the Industrial Revolution?

❸ How did labour costs contribute to the decline of heavy industry?

❹ Why are modern industries described as footloose?

❺ What are the two most important location factors for footloose industry?

Industry in LEDCs

Industrialisation

LEDCs have not gone through an Industrial Revolution in the same way as MEDCs. The majority of the population are still employed in agriculture. Before industrialisation can take place a number of problems need to be overcome:

capital for investment is limited	transport networks are poor and can be disrupted by the weather	government officials may be corrupt	electricity is unreliable or unavailable
local markets are limited		MEDCs may trade unfairly.	lack of skilled labour and management expertise

Formal and informal industry

Industry in LEDCs is divided into **formal** and **informal** sectors. The informal sector employs the most people.

- Formal – official job; workers have contracts, work fixed hours, regular wages. Examples: working in a factory or office.

- Informal – unofficial job; no contract, long irregular hours, uncertain wages. Example: working in a small workshop or on a street stall.

Industry and the environment

All industries have an impact on the environment, especially heavy industries.
- Air – global warming, acid rain, ozone layer damage.

- Land – industrial waste, toxic waste, ugly buildings.
- Water – chemical spills in rivers, oils spills at sea.

Case Study : Environmental impact of a Transnational Corporation (TNC)

- Company – Union Carbide Corporation
- Business – chemical manufacturer
- Location – head office in USA, factories in every continent
- On 2 December 1984 a Union Carbide factory in India was responsible for the world's worst industrial disaster.
- Union Carbide was fined $470 million by the Indian Government.
- Thousands of people remain very sick.

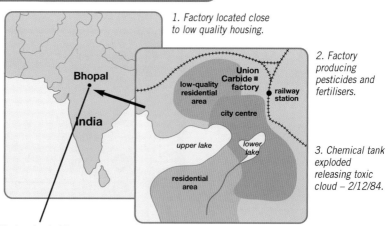

1. Factory located close to low quality housing.

2. Factory producing pesticides and fertilisers.

3. Chemical tank exploded releasing toxic cloud – 2/12/84.

Factory located in city of Bhopal.

5. Twelve thousand killed and 500 000 injured by chemicals.

4. Toxic cloud covered over 40 km² of Bhopal.

Newly Industrialising Countries

A small number of LEDCs have developed economies based on manufacturing since the 1960s. They are known as Newly Industrialising Countries (NICs). NICs include Singapore, Hong Kong, South Korea and Brazil.

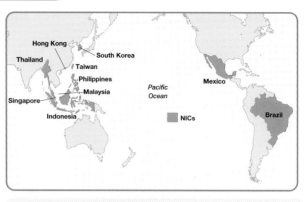

Strategies

Governments of **Newly Industrialising Countries (NICs)** used a range of strategies to achieve industrial development:

- Cheap loans and subsidies were given to new industries.
- Imports were restricted to protect own industries from competition.
- Currencies were devalued to make exports cheaper.

Successes

- Manufacturing industry has progressed from textiles and clothes to high-tech electronics.
- Wages and living standards have risen.
- In some cases, NICs' industries have grown to become transnational companies.

Problems

- Transnational companies move to other countries when subsidies and tax breaks end.
- Wages have risen, making other LEDCs cheaper locations.
- NICs borrowed heavily – many have struggled to repay debts.

Transnational corporations

Transnational Corporations (TNCs), or multinationals, are very large companies, such as Nike, with offices and factories all over the world.

Location of TNCs

TNCs locate in many different countries for several reasons:

- Access is gained to potential new markets.
- Low labour costs in LEDCs = increased profit.
- LEDC governments encourage TNCs with low taxes.

Advantages of TNCs

- Employment is provided, increasing wealth.
- Taxes are paid to the government
- Technology and skills are transferred between countries.

Disadvantages of TNCs

- Profit is transferred to TNC headquarters, usually in MEDCs.
- Wages are low and working conditions sometimes poor.
- TNC activities may cause environmental damage.

KEY TERMS

Make sure you understand these terms before moving on!

- formal
- informal
- Newly Industrialising Countries (NICs)
- Transnational Corporations (TNCs)

QUICK TEST

1. What is an NIC?
2. Why did NICs restrict imports?
3. Name an example of a TNC?
4. Why do transnational companies locate factories in LEDCs?
5. What were the effects of the accident in Bhopal?

Tourism

Tourism is when people visit places for enjoyment. This may be a holiday for a few days or weeks, but must include an overnight stay.

Growth of tourism

Tourism has expanded due to a number of changes in lifestyle since the 1950s:

- Paid holiday – increase in number of weeks paid annual leave.

- Wages – pay has increased faster than rate of inflation ➡ people can afford more holidays.

- Television – increase in number of travel programmes.

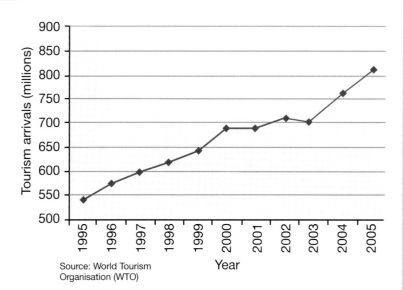

Source: World Tourism Organisation (WTO)

- Adventure – life has generally become safer ➡ people seek adventure and excitement on holiday.

- Older people – increased life expectancy and early retirement means there are more older people wishing to travel.

- Air fares – low-cost airlines and independent travel agents offer more affordable flights.

Tourist destinations

Tourist destinations are places that are attractive to tourists.
Places may be attractive for different reasons:

- Climate – places that are hot and dry make popular destinations for people who want to relax in the sun. In the winter, many mountainous areas with reliable snowfall have become ski resorts.

- Scenery – sightseeing is a favourite tourist activity. Spectacular natural landforms such as mountains, lakes and waterfalls attract tourism.

- **Ecology** – trees, plants and exotic wildlife are an attraction for many people.
  A large number of eco-tourism resorts have been set up in recent years.
  Eco-tourism aims to be environmentally friendly and sustainable.

- **Culture** – many people enjoy experiencing different cultures on holiday. Places with interesting history, architecture, food and music have become popular destinations.

- Activities – many tourist resorts offer activity holidays. These range from the sedate (e.g. ballroom dancing) to the extreme (e.g. bungee jumping).

Case Study: The Lake District, UK

- The Lake District is a **National Park** in North-West England.
- National Parks are large areas of attractive countryside which are protected by law.
- They were established in 1949 to preserve and enhance the beauty of the landscape and to give the public access to the countryside for recreation.
- The Lake District is an upland area created by glaciation. Its combination of hills, lakes, farmland and picturesque towns make it a very attractive place for tourists to visit.

National Parks

Benefits

- The growth of tourism in the Lake District has benefited people living there by providing employment and bringing money into the area.
- Money raised by the National Park Authority has been used to increase the level of protection of and public awareness of the area.

Problems

- Traffic congestion – too many cars and coaches on narrow country roads lead to congestion and an increase in air pollution in the towns. A lack of car parking results in visitors parking in inconsiderate places.
- Soil erosion – the huge numbers of walkers have resulted in footpaths being worn away. During heavy rain this leads to soil erosion and gullying.
- **Honey pots** – areas that attract the most visitors are known as 'honey pots'. The development of honey pots, such as Bowness, is ruining features that made them popular in the first place.

Management

The National Park Authority, and local government, has tried to solve some of the problems caused by tourism:

- car parking has been increased and people are encouraged to use public transport
- footpaths have been reinforced using local stone
- development has been concentrated in 'honey pots' to protect other areas.

 **INTERNET**
Tourism concern
www.tourismconcern.org.uk

KEY TERMS

Make sure you understand these terms before moving on!

- culture
- ecology
- honey pots
- national Park
- tourism

QUICK TEST

1. What is the official definition of tourism?
2. How have changes in working conditions led to an increase in tourism?
3. List the five factors that may make destinations appealing to tourists.
4. How has tourism benefitted people who live in National Parks?
5. What is a honey pot?

Tourism changes

Changing destinations

Tourism in the UK became popular in the 1800s. People who were wealthy enough visited seaside towns such as Brighton. Unfortunately, the unreliable British weather ruined many holidays. During the 1970s the price of air travel fell. Mass tourism began as package holidays to the warm and dry Mediterranean coast became very popular. Package holidays include flights, hotels and food. As more people began to travel abroad for their holidays, the UK resorts declined. Meanwhile, tourism on the Mediterranean coast exploded. Fishing villages in countries such as Portugal, Spain and Greece were taken over by huge concrete hotels.

By the 1990s many Mediterranean destinations had become over-crowded. Their original beauty and culture had disappeared. People began to look for new, unspoilt places to visit. Many Mediterranean resorts began to decline. Today, long-haul destinations such as the USA, parts of Asia and Africa have become popular. However, the tourist industry is always on the look-out for new places to develop.

World's top tourist destinations

Country	Number of tourists in 2004 (million)
France	75
Spain	52
USA	46
China	45
Italy	37
UK	28
Hong Kong	22
Mexico	21
Germany	20
Austria	19

🌐 **INTERNET**
Virtual tourist
http://www.vtourist.com/

Impacts of tourism

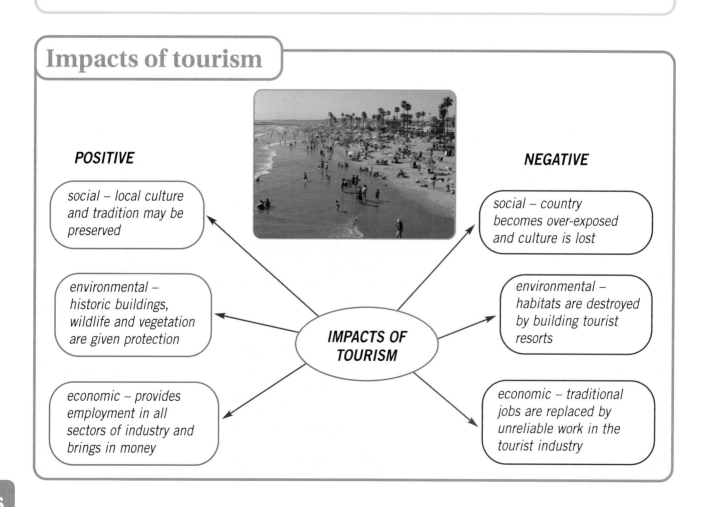

POSITIVE

social – local culture and tradition may be preserved

environmental – historic buildings, wildlife and vegetation are given protection

economic – provides employment in all sectors of industry and brings in money

IMPACTS OF TOURISM

NEGATIVE

social – country becomes over-exposed and culture is lost

environmental – habitats are destroyed by building tourist resorts

economic – traditional jobs are replaced by unreliable work in the tourist industry

Kenya, Africa

- **Kenya** is a country in East Africa.
- It is a LEDC, and the standard of living for many Kenyans is very low compared to people in countries such as the UK.

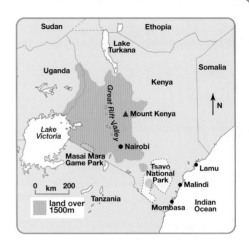

Tourist attractions
- Climate – sunny all year, average temperature 25°C, low rainfall, two rainy seasons.
- Scenery – stunning **savanna** landscapes, Mount Kenya and palm-fringed coral beaches.
- Ecology – over 50 National Parks or game reserves, home to lions, elephants and giraffes.

Benefits
- Around 180 000 Kenyans are employed in hotels, restaurants and as guides. Another 380 000 Kenyans make a living by selling things to tourists or by supplying hotels with food and other supplies.
- The money earned is taxed by the government, and invested in things such as industry, schools and hospitals.

Problems
- Local fisherman have been banned from fishing in the National Maritime Park, near Mombasa.
- Beaches may only be used by hotel guests. Locals are no longer able to collect seafood.
- Coral reefs are dying because tourists walk on the coral and take home pieces as souvenirs.
- The Maasai people have been forced to leave the Game Reserves by the government.
- Tourist minibuses have churned up the soil in the National Parks, causing soil erosion.

Sustainable Tourism and Conservation
In Lamu, a northern coastal town, **sustainable tourism** and **conservation** is being adopted. Sustainable tourism encourages smaller groups of more wealthy tourists, and tries to limit impacts on the environment.
- Hotels are only allowed to be built if they are to be no higher than the palm trees.
- Tourists are educated about local culture and customs using simple notice boards.
- Tourists staying in Lamu pay a tax, which is used to conserve and repair traditional buildings.

Make sure you understand these terms before moving on!
- conservation
- Kenya
- savanna
- sustainable tourism

QUICK TEST
1. What type of holiday became popular in the 1800s?
2. What type of holiday became popular in the 1970s?
3. Why do governments of LEDCs encourage tourism?
4. Describe Kenya's climate.
5. What is meant by sustainable tourism?

Resources

- Resources are any parts of the environment that are used by people to live.
- World population growth, and improvements in standards of living, have increased the rate at which resources are being used.

Resources

Resources may either be **renewable** or **non-renewable**.

Renewable
- Renewable resources include water, trees and soil.
- These resources should last for ever if they are used carefully.
- Unfortunately, even many renewable resources are being used up faster than they can be replaced.

Non-renewable
- Non-renewable resources include coal, oil, gas and minerals.
- These resources are in limited supply – once they have been used up they cannot be replaced.
- Non-renewable resources are being used up at an increasingly fast rate.

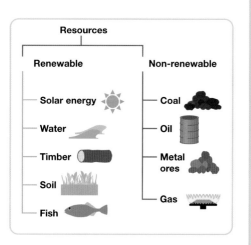

Resource depletion

The Earth's resources are being depleted (running out) for two key reasons:

Population growth
- The world's population is over six billion.
- The world's population will increase by another three billion over the next 50 years.
- The more people there are, the more resources are needed.

Development
- Development means improvements in wealth and standards of living.
- The majority of the world's population live in poorer countries (LEDCs).
- As LEDCs develop, the demand for consumer goods fuelled by materialism is rising, increasing the pressure on limited resources.

Resource substitution

- **Resource substitution** means replacing one resource with another.
- Some people believe that technological advances mean that if any resources run out we will be able to replace them with alternatives.
- An example is cars running on alcohol instead of petrol.

Sustainable development

- To prevent the world's resources from being depleted it is necessary to adopt policies of sustainable development and conservation.
- **Sustainable development** – meeting our needs today without compromising the ability of future generations to meet their needs.
- Conservation – managing and protecting natural resources to prevent them running out.

Agenda 21

- Governments of 153 countries agreed a policy of sustainable development at the Earth Summit in Rio de Janeiro, Brazil in 1992.
- An important part of the agreement is Agenda 21 which aims to achieve sustainable development at a local level. An example of local sustainable development is kerbside collection of recycleable waste.

Recycling and waste

- **Recycling** reduces the amount of waste, conserves resources and reduces pollution.
- It includes turning waste into new products, or just re-using things.
- It is possible to recycle 70% of domestic waste.
- The UK recycles just 8% of its waste.
- In the UK we throw away 25 million tonnes of household waste per year.
- Landfill sites receive 83% of our waste.
- Incinerator plants receive 9% of our waste.
- Burying and burning this much waste uses up precious resources.
- Landfill sites may contain dangerous chemicals, which can leak into water supplies.
- Incinerating waste may release dangerous chemicals into the atmosphere.

glass • paper • car batteries • plastic • aluminium • textiles • steel • organic waste

INTERNET
Planet.com
www.channel4.com/learning/microsites/P/planet/menu.html

KEY TERMS

Make sure you understand these terms before moving on!
- agenda 21
- non-renewable
- recycling
- renewable
- resource substitution
- resources
- sustainable development
- waste

QUICK TEST

1. What is a resource?
2. What are the two key reasons for resource depletion?
3. What is resource substitution?
4. What is Agenda 21?
5. Where does the majority of our domestic waste end up?

Energy and the environment

- People need energy to run machines and to provide heat and light.
- The global demand for energy is increasing every year.

Resources and consumption

Energy resources and energy demand are not evenly distributed around the world.

- MEDCs consume 80% of the total energy produced, but have only 25% of the world's population.
- LEDCs rarely have significant known energy reserves – those that do, often export them to MEDCs.
- In some MEDCs energy demand is slowly decreasing due to more efficient cars and household appliances.
- Global energy use is expected to increase up to 50% by 2020, as a result of population growth and economic development.

The average American uses 35 times more energy than the average Indian.

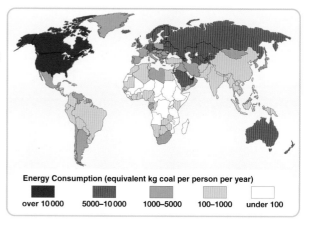

Energy Consumption (equivalent kg coal per person per year)

| over 10 000 | 5000–10 000 | 1000–5000 | 100–1000 | under 100 |

Non-renewable and renewable energy

Energy resources are divided into two categories:
- Non-renewable – resources that will run out one day (finite).
- Renewable – resources that are continually renewed and will not run out.

  90% of the world's energy comes from fossil fuels (coal, oil and gas).

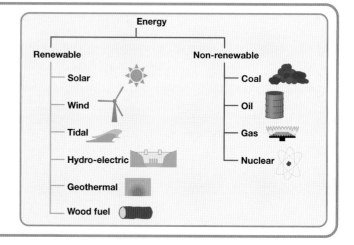

Wind power

- Wind energy may be captured by wind turbines. Rotor blades are angled to face the wind ➡ wind turns rotor blades at up to 400 km per hour ➡ generator converts energy into electricity.
- Wind power is most suitable for upland and offshore areas with reliable strong winds, especially if they are a long way from the main electricity grid. Example – Denmark is the major user of wind power.
- Advantages – no greenhouse gases, electricity is cheap, it is adaptable (from one turbine for an isolated house, to a wind farm with hundreds of turbines).
- Disadvantages – perceived by some as visually intrusive in areas of natural beauty, rotor blades are noisy and may interfere with television signals, to replace fossil fuels would need a huge number of turbines.

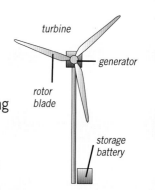

turbine

generator

rotor blade

storage battery

Global warming

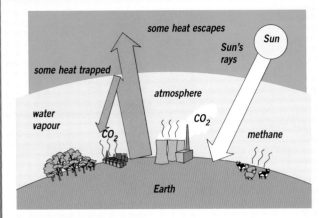

Greenhouse effect

The **greenhouse effect** describes the way in which the Earth's atmosphere traps heat from the Sun.

- Solar energy reaches the Earth as light.
- Earth's surface re-radiates energy as heat.
- Atmospheric gases including water vapour, **carbon dioxide** (CO_2) and **methane** absorb the heat, keeping the surface of the Earth warm.

Evidence of global warming

- Average global temperature has increased by 0.6°C in the past 100 years.
- Ice cores taken from the Antarctic ice sheet show that the amount of CO_2 and methane in the atmosphere has increased.

Possible causes

- **Fossil fuels** – each year 5000 million tonnes of CO_2 are released into the atmosphere when fossil fuels are burned in power stations, factories and cars.
- Deforestation – trees convert CO_2 into oxygen. Most temperate forests have been felled. Tropical rainforests are now being cut down.
- Methane – methane gas is being added to the atmosphere by bacteria in rice fields, rotting waste in rubbish dumps, and by flatulent cattle.

Possible effects on the UK

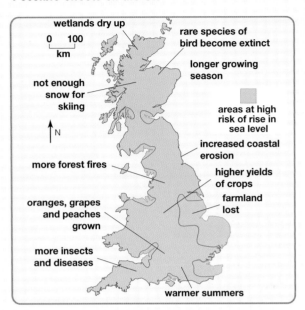

Reducing CO_2

Reducing the amount of CO_2 that there is in the atmosphere may be achieved by the following:

- Cutting down emissions – Earth Summit agreement (Kyoto 1997).
- Stopping deforestation and increasing tree planting programmes.
- Slowing population growth ➡ less fossil fuels will be needed.

Controversy

Not all scientists agree that global warming is being caused by people. They argue that:

- Earth's climate has always fluctuated between ice ages and hotter periods due to variations in the Earth's rotation around the Sun. For example, Europe experienced a 'mini ice-age' between 1300 and 1800.

KEY TERMS

Make sure you understand these terms before moving on!

- carbon dioxide
- energy
- fossil fuels
- greenhouse effect
- methane

QUICK TEST

1. Why is energy demand decreasing in some MEDCs?
2. Why is global energy use expected to rise by 50% over the next 20 years?
3. What areas are suitable for wind power?
4. What is the greenhouse effect?
5. What may be causing global warming?

Development

Development is the use of resources and technology to increase wealth and improve standards of living.

Contrasts in development

- The richer countries are known as More Economically Developed Countries (**MEDCs**).
- The poorer countries are known as Less Economically Developed Countries (**LEDCs**).
- MEDCs have only 20% of the world's population, but own 80% of the world's wealth.
- MEDCs are mainly in the northern hemisphere – USA, Canada, Western Europe and Japan.
- LEDCs are mainly in the southern hemisphere – continents of South America, Africa and Asia.

Terms such as MEDC and LEDC hide the range of **development** – many countries are somewhere in the middle.

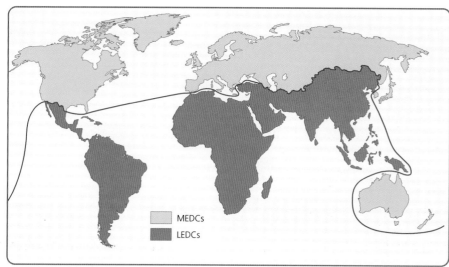

MEDCs
LEDCs

Obstacles to development

LEDCs are frequently trapped in a cycle of underdevelopment. The obstacles they face prevent them from developing.

Less Economically Developed Country

few manufactured exports, many people cannot read and write, illness

not enough money to invest in industries, schools and hospitals

lack of industry, poor education and healthcare

Hazards
- Natural hazards such as droughts, floods, earthquakes, volcanic eruptions and tropical storms are more common in LEDCs.

- Buildings may be poorly built and unable to withstand hazards.
- LEDCs lack resources to deal with the after effects of hazards.
- Money must be spent of rebuilding, rather than development projects.

Water
- 1.2 billion people in LEDCs do not have access to a safe water supply.
- Contaminated water causes disease such as cholera, dysentery and diarrhoea.
- Sick people are unable to work, and place a strain on healthcare services.
- Access to water is poor ➡ hours may be spent collecting water from wells.

Measuring development

Development indicators give a measure of a country's level of development.

Economic Development

- Economic development is measured using **Gross National Product** (GNP).
- GNP per capita is the total value of all goods and services produced by a country in one year, divided by the population to give an average per person.

Social Development

Social development is measured using population data:

- **Birth rate** – number of live births per thousand people per year.
- **Death rate** – number of deaths per thousand people per year.
- Life expectancy – average life span in years.

Human Development Index (HDI)

Human Development Index (HDI) takes into account economic and social development:

- Income per person – adjusted for the cost of living.
- Education – percentage of adults who are literate, and average number of years in education.
- Life expectancy.
- HDI is recorded as a score from 0 to 1, with 1 being the most developed.

Rank	Country	HDI
1	Canada	0.932
2	Norway	0.927
3	USA	0.927
4	Japan	0.924
5	Belgium	0.923
170	Burundi	0.324
171	Burkina Faso	0.304
172	Ethiopia	0.298
172	Niger	0.298
174	Sierra Leone	0.254

Development projects

Development projects are schemes that promote development in LEDCs.

Prestige projects

Prestige projects are large-scale, expensive schemes such as building dams, power stations, airports and roads. These schemes look impressive but may cause problems:

- Money borrowed to fund project increases country's debt.
- Poor may be displaced to provide land for project.
- Maintenance is expensive ➡ project may run out of money.
  Example – Aswan Dam, Egypt.

Appropriate technology projects

Appropriate technology projects are small scale and involve local people, for example, providing wells and toilets. This type of scheme has several advantages:

- Low-technology projects are cheaper and there is less to go wrong.
- Projects provide employment for local people.
- Local people are able to afford products.
  Example – Tube wells in Bangladesh.

 INTERNET
UN Cyber School Bus
http://www.un.org/pubs/cyberschoolbus/index.html

KEY TERMS

- birth rate
- death rate
- development
- Gross National Product (GNP)
- Human Development Index
- LEDCs
- MEDCs

QUICK TEST

1. What is development?
2. In which hemisphere are most MEDCs located?
3. What is the HDI and what does it try to do?
4. Why does a poor water supply limit development?
5. What are the characteristics of an appropriate technology development project?

Trade and aid

Trade

- International trade is the exchange of goods and services between countries.
- Trade happens when a producing country is able to sell goods or services more cheaply, or of better quality, than the consuming country.
- **Imports** are goods bought by a country.
- **Exports** are goods sold by a country.
- **Balance of trade** is the difference between the value of the imports and exports.

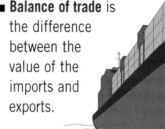

Fair trade

Fair trade is a way of doing business that ensures the people who produce the goods benefit.

Benefits
- Minimum wages and safe working conditions.
- Restrictions on child labour.
- Protection for the environment.
- 'Fair trade' products can be bought in most supermarkets in the UK.

INTERNET

Fair Trade
http://www.fairtrade.org.uk/
Oxfam
http://www.oxfam.org.uk/

Pattern of world trade

MEDCs make much more money from trade than LEDCs. Why is this?
- LEDCs export raw materials (crops, timber, ores) to MEDCs.
- MEDCs export manufactured and processed goods (processed food, vehicles, electronics) to LEDCs.
- Raw materials have much less value than manufactured goods.

Percentage of total exports
Primary products
Over 75%   50–75%
Manufactured products
Over 75%   50–75%   No data

Advantages for MEDCs
- The price of manufactured goods has increased steadily.
- MEDCs are becoming richer so are able to import more raw materials from LEDCs.
- Competition between LEDCs ensures MEDCs can buy goods for the lowest possible price.

Disadvantages for LEDCs
- The price of raw materials has fallen compared to the price of manufactured goods. LEDCs cannot afford to import the manufactured goods they need.
- Price of raw materials is not stable. When there is a surplus, prices fall and LEDCs earn even less.
- Increases dependency of LEDCs on MEDCs.

Aid

- Aid is a transfer of resources from a MEDC to a LEDC.
- Aid includes money, equipment, food, training, skilled people and loans.

Donors and recipients
- The United Nations recommends countries spend 0.7% of GNP on aid per year – few do.
- Largest donors are Norway, Denmark and Sweden.
- Largest recipients are China, Egypt and Indonesia.

Types of aid

- Emergency aid – short-term immediate relief during or after disaster, e.g. famine or earthquake. Includes blankets, tents, medicine, food, clothes, water and equipment.
- Long-term aid – aims to increase development and improve standard of living. Includes education, training, technology and improvements to infrastructure.

- Multilateral aid – arranged by international organisations: International Monetary Fund (IMF), United Nations (UN) and World Bank.
- Bilateral aid – an arrangement between individual governments.
- Tied aid – recipient government must agree to spend money on goods from donor country.
- NGO aid – Non-Governmental Organisations are charities such as Oxfam that run aid projects. Money is raised through private donations and government grants.

Advantages and disadvantages of aid

Advantages
- **Aid** can be beneficial to MEDCs and LEDCs.
- Emergency aid saves lives.
- Long-term aid can improve the standard of living of people living in LEDCs.
- Tied aid boosts exports and secures jobs in MEDCs, e.g. arms industry.
- Aid can open markets for goods from MEDCs, e.g. food aid.

Disadvantages
- Aid is frequently in the form of a loan and LEDCs sink further into debt.
- Food aid may cause local prices to fall and put local farmers out of business.
- Tied aid may force LEDCs to buy inappropriate technology, e.g. combine harvesters.
- Corrupt officials may pocket aid or rich landowners may benefit more than poorer farmers.
- Large-scale infrastructure projects damage the environment and increase the national debt.

KEY TERMS

Make sure you understand these terms before moving on!
- aid
- balance of trade
- exports
- fair trade
- imports

QUICK TEST

1. What is trade?
2. What is meant by the term balance of trade?
3. Describe the pattern of trade between MEDCs and LEDCs.
4. What is fair trade?
5. How does tied aid benefit MEDCs?

Practice questions

Use the questions to test your progress.
Check your answers on page 95.

Population

1. Name the model shown in Figure 1. (1 mark)

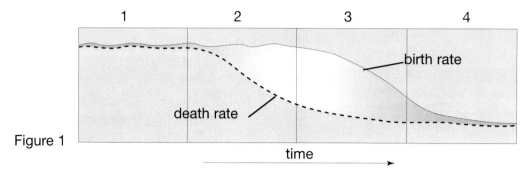

Figure 1

....

2. Describe what is happening at stage 2. (3 marks)

....

....

3. Some MEDCs have entered a fifth stage of the model. What does this mean? (3 marks)

....

....

4. Name two areas outside of the UK with a low population density. (2 marks)

....

....

5. Explain how physical factors may result in low population density. (4 marks)

....

....

....

6. What information is shown on a population pyramid? (4 marks)

....

....

....

7. Describe two ways in which the population pyramid for an MEDC is different to that of an LEDC. (2 marks)

....

....

....

8. Using an example you have studied describe the causes and effects of a large scale migration of people. (6 marks)

....

....

....

Settlement

1. What is meant by the term urbanisation? (1 mark)

....

2. Label the zones A, B and C on Figure 2. (3 marks)

C

A

Figure 2

B

Urban land use model for an LEDC

3. What are shanty towns? (2 marks)

....

4. Using an example you have studied, describe how shanty towns can be improved. (4 marks)

....

....

....

5. How are land use zones in LEDCs different from MEDCs? (2 marks)

....

....

6. Describe the characteristics of a CBD in an MEDC. (3 marks)

....

....

7. Describe the problems caused by the decline of inner cities in MEDCs. (4 marks)

....

....

8. Using an example you have studied, explain how inner city areas may be improved. (6 marks)

....

....

....

....

/50

Practice questions

Use the questions to test your progress.
Check your answers on page 95.

Agriculture

1. Label the types of farming A, B and C on Figure 1. (3 marks)

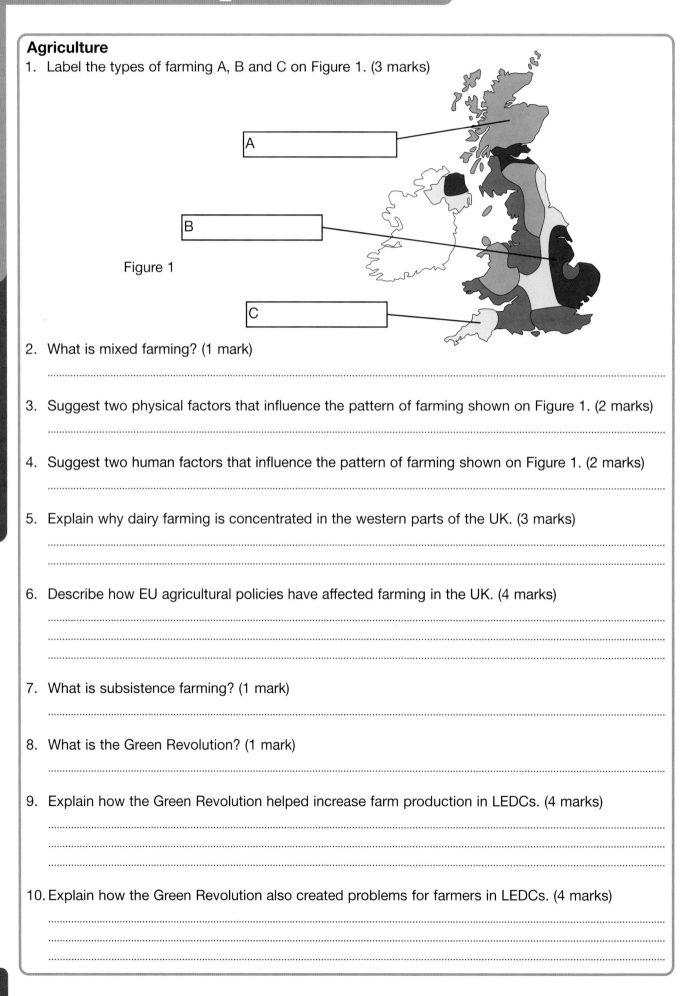

A

B

Figure 1

C

2. What is mixed farming? (1 mark)

....

3. Suggest two physical factors that influence the pattern of farming shown on Figure 1. (2 marks)

....

4. Suggest two human factors that influence the pattern of farming shown on Figure 1. (2 marks)

....

5. Explain why dairy farming is concentrated in the western parts of the UK. (3 marks)

....
....

6. Describe how EU agricultural policies have affected farming in the UK. (4 marks)

....
....
....

7. What is subsistence farming? (1 mark)

....

8. What is the Green Revolution? (1 mark)

....

9. Explain how the Green Revolution helped increase farm production in LEDCs. (4 marks)

....
....
....

10. Explain how the Green Revolution also created problems for farmers in LEDCs. (4 marks)

....
....
....

Industry

1. What is primary industry? (1 mark)

   ....

2. How are primary, secondary and tertiary industries linked? (2 marks)

   ....

3. Figure 2 shows the employment structures of three countries at different stages of economic development. Match the employment structures in the table below. (3 marks)

   Figure 2

More Economically Developed Country	
Less Economically Developed Country	
Newly Industrialised Country	

4. Give two reasons why employment structures can change. (2 marks)

   ....

5. For an industry you have studied, explain how raw materials, labour and markets have influenced its location. (6 marks)

   ....

   ....

   ....

   ....

6. What is a transnational company? (1 mark)

   ....

7. In what ways do governments of LEDCs influence the location of transnational companies ? (4 marks)

   ....

   ....

   ....

8. Using an example you have studied, explain the advantages and disadvantages of transnational companies to LEDCs. (6 marks)

   ....

   ....

   ....

   ....

   /50

How well did you do? X 1-12 Start again   13-26 Getting there   27-38 Good work   39-50 Excellent! ✓

89

Practice questions

Use the questions to test
your progress.
Check your answers on page 95.

Managing Resources

1. Figure 1 shows the world growth in energy consumption. Which resource provided the largest amount of energy in 1995? (1 mark)

....

Figure 1

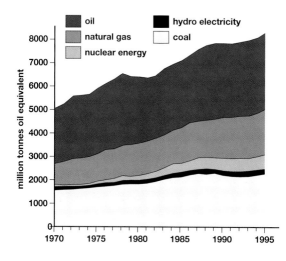

World growth in energy consumption

2. Which source of energy increased most between 1970 and 1995? (1 mark)

....

3. Describe the change in total energy consumption between 1970 and 1995. (3 marks)

....

....

4. Explain why energy consumption is expected to increase by 50% by 2020. (4 marks)

....

....

5. What can countries do to manage increasing demands for energy? (6 marks)

....

....

....

....

6. Name two attractions of a tourist destination you have studied. (2 marks)

....

7. Describe the advantages that tourism brought to an area you have studied. (3 marks)

....

....

8. How can tourism be developed, while protecting the environment? (5 marks)

....

....

....

....

Development

1. What is the meaning of Gross National Product (GNP) per capita? (1 mark)

....

2. Why is GNP on its own not an accurate way to measure levels of development? (2 marks)

....

3. Give two other ways that the level of development of a country can be measured. (2 marks)

....

4. Using an example you have studied, explain how a poor water supply can make it difficult for a country to develop. (4 marks)

....

....

5. What percentage of GNP should be donated as aid according to the United Nations? (1 mark)

....

6. Name the countries which exceed the UN target in Figure 2. (3 marks)

....

....

Figure 2

Aid as a percentage of GNP

7. Name and describe two different types of overseas aid. (4 marks)

....

....

....

8. Give three disadvantages of aid to the receiving country. (3 marks)

....

....

9. How does international trade benefit MEDCs more than LEDCs? (5 marks)

....

....

/50

How well did you do? ✗ 1-12 Start again   13-26 Getting there   27-38 Good work   39-50 Excellent! ✓

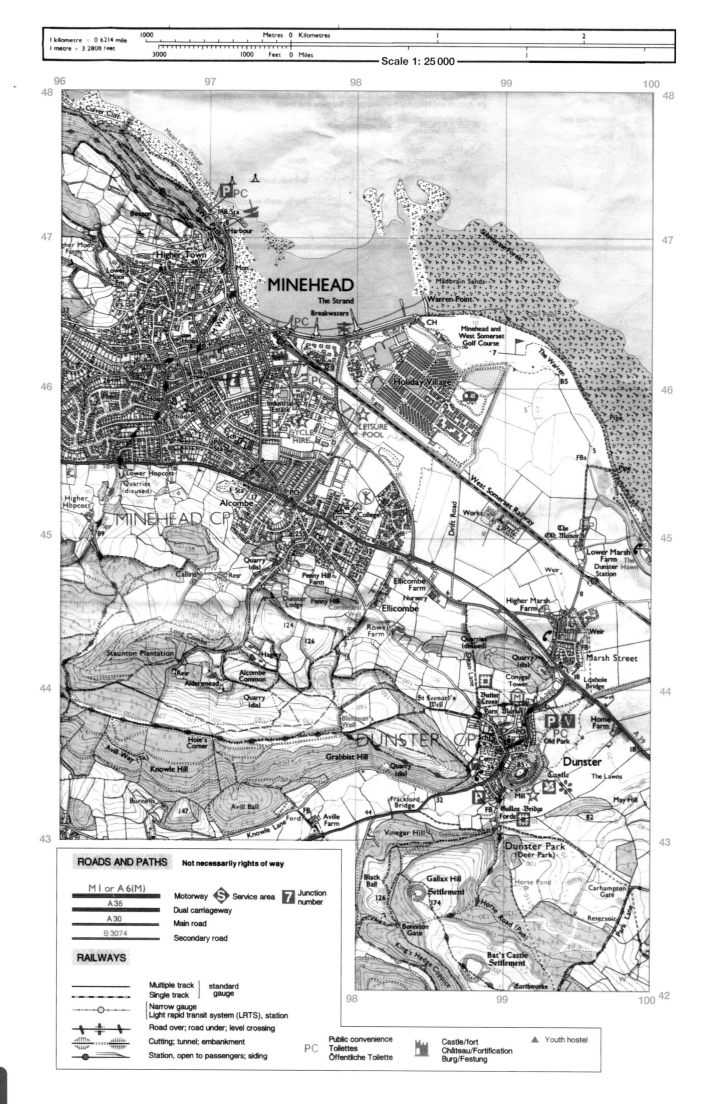

Scale 1: 25 000

ROADS AND PATHS Not necessarily rights of way

M 1 or A 6(M)   Motorway   S Service area   7 Junction number

A 35   Dual carriageway

A 30   Main road

B 3074   Secondary road

RAILWAYS

Multiple track } standard
Single track   } gauge

Narrow gauge
Light rapid transit system (LRTS), station

Road over; road under; level crossing

Cutting; tunnel; embankment

Station, open to passengers; siding

PC   Public convenience
Toilettes
Öffentliche Toilette

Castle/fort
Château/Fortification
Burg/Festung

▲ Youth hostel

Tectonic activity
Quick Test Answers

Page 5 The Earth's Crust
1. Oceanic and continental
2. Heat from core causes convection currents in mantle. Movements in mantle drag tectonic plates.
3. Tectonic plates move away from each other.
4. On destructive and collision boundaries.
5. Destructive

Page 7 Earthquakes
1. Focus is point underground where energy is released, epicentre is surface directly above focus.
2. Seismometer
3. Earthquake damage
4. Weaker buildings and lack of resources to deal with secondary effects.
5. Secondary effect

Page 9 Volcanoes
1. One that has erupted in last 2000 years, but not recently.
2. Constructive and destructive.
3. Formed from layers of lava and ash.
4. Monitoring the temperature and shape of volcanoes.
5. Fertile soils, geothermal energy, tourism, minerals.

Rocks and Landscapes
Quick Test Answers

Page 11 Rocks
1. Igneous
2. Shells of tiny sea creatures.
3. Temperatures must go above and then below freezing.
4. Steep side of a chalk escarpment.
5. Pervious

Page 13 Landscapes
1. A large intrusion of igneous rock which cooled inside the Earth's crust.
2. Tors.
3. Tourism and china clay mining.
4. Limestone surface is weathered along joints.
5. Stalactites hang down, stalagmites rise up.

River Landscapes
Quick Test Answers

Page 15 River processes
1. Continuous cycling of water between land, sea and atmosphere.
2. Trees, plants and buildings.
3. When surface is impermeable or soil is saturated.
4. Hydraulic power, corrasion, corrosion, attrition.
5. There is less friction from bed and banks.

Page 17 River landforms
1. e.g. High Force, River Tees, UK.
2. Gorge
3. Point bar
4. Middle course
5. Raised river bank made from alluvium.

Page 19 Flooding
1. Flash flood.
2. Impermeable surfaces increase run-off.
3. Hard engineering aims to prevent flooding, soft engineering aims to help people cope with floods.
4. Preventing building on a flood plain.
5. Increases interception and evapotranspiration reducing run-off.

Glacial Landscapes
Quick Test Answers

Page 21 Glaciation
1. 10000 years ago
2. The glacier melts.
3. Plucking, abrasion and freeze–thaw.
4. Steep slopes, high rainfall and snowmelt.
5. Deforestation to make ski-runs increases avalanches.

Page 23 Glacial landforms
1. Less erosion as glacier is moving uphill.
2. Arête
3. Hanging valleys formed where small glaciers joined major one.
4. River spurs which were worn away by glacial erosion.
5. Glacial deposition of till, while the glacier was moving.

Coastal Landscapes
Quick Test Answers

Page 25 Coastal processes
1. Wind – friction between wind and the sea
2. Fetch – the distance travelled by the wind
3. Constructive wave
4. Rocks containing calcium carbonate – chalk and limestone
5. Longshore drift

Page 27 Coastal landforms
1. Granite cliffs
2. Stack
3. Base of coastal cliffs
4. Beach and spit
5. Salt-marsh

Page 29 Coastal management
1. Trapping material to build up the beach.
2. To reflect wave energy.
3. Allowing sea to erode and flood the land.
4. Department of Environment, Food and Rural Affairs, and the local authority.
5. By depriving other areas of beach material.

Weather and Climate
Quick Test Answers

Page 31 Weather
1. Sinking air
2. Air warms as it sinks ⟹ clouds evaporate ⟹ little rain.
3. Summer
4. Light winds, sunshine, low temperatures and frost.
5. Anticlockwise

Page 33 Climate
1. Weather is the condition of the air at a certain time; climate is the average weather over a period of time.
2. Sun's rays have further to travel and are more spread out.
3. Atmosphere becomes thinner.
4. Climate influenced by the sea
5. Temperatures inland are not influenced by cool sea water.

Page 35 Weather and people
1. Late summer and autumn.
2. Tropical areas either side of the equator.
3. Low air pressure causes sea levels to rise.
4. A long, continuous period of dry weather.
5. A lack of rainfall caused by high air pressure.

Ecosystems
Quick Test Answers

Page 37 Ecosystems
1. Sunlight, temperature and rainfall.
2. Trees that shed leaves, shrubs and grasses.
3. Africa, S. America, Australia.
4. Fast growing, die back in dry season, spreading roots.
5. Nomadic pasturalism

Page 39 Global environments
1. Evergreen, conical shape, flexible branches, waxy needles, thick bark.
2. Podsol soil.
3. Equator, Brazil, West Africa, S.E. Asia.
4. High temperatures of 27°C and rainfall all year.
5. Trees have buttress roots and drip tips on leaves.

Geographical Skills
Quick Test Answers

Page 41 Map skills
1. 4 cm
2. 1: 25000 map
3. 1 km²
4. Public house
5. Contour lines, spot heights and triangulation points.

Answers to practice questions
Page 42 Tectonic activity
1. Composite Volcano (1)
2. A = crater (1) B = magma chamber (1) C = vent (1)
3. Destructive plate boundaries (1), explosive eruption (1), builds up in layers of ash (1), and layers of lava (1).
4. Pyroclastic flow (1), mud flow (1), lava flow (1), ash fall (1), global cooling (1).
5. Both occur on plate boundaries (1), plate movement causes earthquakes and volcanic eruptions (1).
6. Named case study (1), type of plate boundary (1), pressure builds up (1), movement prevented by friction (1), crust snaps along a fault (1), plates move (1), stored energy released (1), ground shaken by seismic waves (1).

7. Fertile soils (1), from weathered ash and lava (1), geothermal energy (1), from steam (1), tourism (1), to see geysers, mud pools etc (1), minerals (1), gold and diamonds etc. (1).
8. Alps, Andes, Himalayas, Rockies (1)
9. Farming (1), Hydro-electric power (1), Tourism (1), Quarrying (1)

Page 43 Rocks and landscapes
1. Igneous (1)
2. Formed from particles of other rocks (1), or from remains of sea creatures (1), contain fossils (1), formed in layers, bedding planes (1)
3. Formed from other rocks (1), during volcanic activity (1), causing extreme heat (1), or earth movements (1), causing extreme pressure (1)
4. Freeze–thaw weathering (1)
5. Water seeps into crack (1), temperature falls below 0°C and water freezes (1), ice expands (1), pressure causes crack to widen. (1)
6. Limestone is made of calcium carbonate (1), which is dissolved by acidic rainwater (1), limestone surface is weathered along joints (1), to form large gaps called grikes (1), remaining blocks of stone are called clints (1).
7. Agriculture (1), tourism (1), quarrying (1), settlement (1)
8. Named area e.g. Dartmoor (1), upland area (1), result of an igneous intrusion (1), called a batholith (1), rocky outcrops (1), called tors (1), 5 to 10 metres high (1), granite is impermeable (1), therefore lots of rivers (1), and marshes (1), area used for sheep and cattle grazing (1), and china clay quaries (1).

Page 44 River landscapes
1. A = mouth (1) B = watershed (1) C = confluence (1)
2. Traction (1), saltation (1), suspension (1), solution (1)
3. Flood plain (1), delta (1), levée (1), point bar (1)
4. Upper course = narrow V-shaped valley (1), middle course = wider U-shaped valley (1), lower course = wide flat valley (1)
5. Heavy rainfall (1), melting snow (1), deforestation (1), urbanisation (1)
6. Forestry (1), sheep farming (1), Hydro-electric power (1), tourism (1), settlement (1)
7. Begins with a large meander (1), narrow neck of land is eroded (1), especially during a flood (1), river takes shortest course through new channel (1), deposition occurs (1), meander is cut-off (1), to form a horseshoe shaped lake (1), over time the lake will silt up. (1)

Page 45 Glacial landscapes
1. A = corrie (1), B = waterfall/ hanging valley (1), C = finger/ribbon lake (1)
2. Freeze–thaw (1), ice expands fracturing rock (1), plucking (1), ice melts, re-freezes and pulls away rocks (1), abrasion (1), plucked rocks grind the surrounding valley (1).
3. Snow collects in hollows (1), is compacted and turns to ice (1), begins to move down hill under own weight (1), erosion steepens corrie sides (1) and deepens corrie floor (1), lip forms at edge of corrie (1), as there is less erosion (1), a lake forms in the corrie after the glacier has melted. (1)
4. Glacial till (1), fine clay (1), rocks (1), boulders (1), unsorted material (1)
5. Two glaciers merge together (1), lateral moraine combines to form medial moraine (1)
6. Tourism (1), skiing (1), Hydro-electric power (1), sheep farming (1), forestry (1), settlement (1)
7. Examples include : encouraging the use of public transport (1), reinforcing footpaths (1), limiting house purchases to local people (1), concentrating tourist development in 'honeypots', hotels built to blend in with environment (1)

Page 46 Coastal landscapes
1. Constructive waves (1)
2. A = headland (1), B = stack (1), C = arch (1)
3. Hydraulic action (1), corrasion/abrasion (1), attrition (1), corrosion (1)
4. Erosion of headland (1), fault in rock eroded by waves (1), fault widens to form crack (1), crack is eroded to form a cave (1), caves break through headland to form arch (1), arch collapses to form a stack. (1)
5. Beach (1), spit (1), bar (1) tombolo (1)
6. Groynes (1), sea walls (1), rock armour (1), cliff stabilisation (1), beach nourishment (1), gabions (1) tetrapods (1)
7. Waves approach beach at oblique angles (1), backwash returns to sea at right angles (1), material is transported along the beach. (1)
8. Fishing (1), tourism (1), settlement (1), industry (1)

Page 47 Weather and climate
1. Depression (1)
2. A = warm front (1), B = cold front (1), C = warm sector (1)
3. Sunny/clear skies (1), cold (1), gentle winds (1), foggy (1)
4. Relief rainfall (1)
5. Air cools as it rises over high land (1), water vapour condenses, forms clouds and rains (1), air warms as it sinks to lower land (1), remaining clouds evaporate and there is little rain. (1)
6. The sun is directly above the equator (1), solar energy at the equator has less distance to travel (1), solar energy at the equator is more concentrated (1), solar energy at the equator

has less atmosphere to pass through. (1)
7. High temperatures all year (1), average 27°C (1), high humidity (1), resulting in daily convectional rainfall (1)
8. Injury or death (1), loss of homes (1), loss of possessions (1), loss of crops (1), psychological damage (1), some people benefit e.g. builders (1)

Page 48 Ecosystems
1. A community of trees, plants, animals and insects living in a particular environment. (1)
2. A wide band between 50°N and the Arctic Circle (1), northern Europe, Siberia, USA and Canada (1)
3. Podsol (1)
4. Heavy rainfall (1), washes nutrients out of soil. (1)
5. Conical shape so snow slides off (1), springy branches so they can support weight of snow (1), seeds protected in cones (1), evergreen to allow efficient photosynthesis (1), thin waxy needles limit moisture loss. (1)
6. Amazon (1), West Africa (1), South-East Asia (1)
7. Agriculture (1), forest cleared for farmland (1), settlement (1), land is needed to provide homes (1), ranching (1), forest cleared to graze cattle (1), logging (1), timber for building and export (1), mining (1), for mineral such as gold, iron ore and bauxite (1), roads (1), to improve communications. (1)
8. Temperatures of 25°C (1), throughout the year (1), wet and dry seasons (1), wet when Sun is overhead (1).
9. Thick bark (1), to protect from fire (1), small waxy leaves (1), leaves dropped in dry season (1), to reduce water loss (1), extra-long roots (1), to reach water table (1)

Page 49 Geographical skills
1. Railway station.
2. South east.
3. 3 to 3.2 (1) km (1)
4. 2 to 2.2 (1) km (1)
5. 973 (1) 442 (1)
6. 85 (1) metres (1)
7. Tourist information centre (1), cycle hire (1), caravan park (1), holiday centre (1), leisure pool (1).
8. Holiday village (1), caravan park (1), residential (1), railway line (1), farmland (1), works (1) secondary road (1) college (1) not leisure pool.
9. Square 9945 is flat (1) and only 5m above sea level (1), square 9743 is hilly (1) and between 40 and 220 metres above sea level (1).
10. At risk from flooding from sea (1), land is poorly drained/marshy (1), suggested by names of farms e.g. Lower Marsh Farm (1), building may not be allowed to protect environment (1).

Population
Quick Test Answers
Page 51 Population
1. Distribution = spread of population; density = how crowded an area is.

2. Densely populated
3. Rapid population growth since 1800.
4. Population would fall.

Page 53 Population change
1. High birth rates and falling death rates.
2. Stage 4
3. 16 to 64
4. More males than females; increasing numbers of older people.
5. The make-up of a population in terms of age, sex and life expectancy.

Page 55 Migration
1. People leaving a country.
2. Increase in the percentage of people living in urban areas.
3. Movement from urban areas to the countryside.
4. Economic and social reasons.
5. War, persecution or natural disasters.

Settlement
Quick Test Answers
Page 57 Settlement
1. Site is the exact location of a settlement, situation is the location of the settlement in relation to the surrounding area.
2. Social and economic activities of a settlement.
3. Mega-city
4. Range
5. Supermarket

Page 59 Settlement in MEDCs
1. The Industrial Revolution
2. Central Business District
3. Urbanisation = increase in the percentage of people living in urban areas; urban growth = the expansion of urban areas
4. The CBD and transition zone.
5. Land becomes cheaper.

Page 61 Settlement in LEDCs
1. City with a population of over 1 million.
2. Rural–urban migration and population growth.
3. Low-quality, self-built housing.
4. City outskirts and poor quality land.
5. Encouraged transnational companies to locate in Jakarta.

Agriculture
Quick Test Answers
Page 63 Agriculture
1. Inputs = soil, climate; processes = harvesting, grazing; outputs = crops, profit
2. Temperature decreases by 6°C every 1 000 metres of altitude.
3. Government limit on maximum production.
4. Subsistence produces food for farmer and family, commercial aims to make profit.
5. East and South-East England, East Scotland.

Page 65 Agricultural change
1. Development of business initiatives other than farming.
2. Nitrates cause algae to grow ⇨ uses up oxygen ⇨ kills fish
3. To make fields bigger and improve access for large farm machinery.
4. Introduction of capital-intensive farming methods in LEDCs.

5. They could not afford HYV seeds and chemicals.

Page 67 Agricultural cases studies
1. Merthyr Farm, Harlech, Snowdonia, Wales
2. Sitio Batol Farm, Luzon, Philippines
3. Income from EU subsidies and grants
4. Land is very expensive

Industry
Quick Test Answers
Page 69 Industry
1. Primary = miner; secondary = baker; tertiary = teacher; quaternary = software developer
2. Location of industry in an area, although it may no longer be the most economic location.
3. Inputs = energy, labour; processes = assembling, packaging; outputs = finished product, waste
4. Primary = 5% Secondary = 30% Tertiary = 65%
5. MEDC – tertiary high, primary low

Page 71 Industry in MEDCs
1. Mechanisation using steam power.
2. Coal
3. Lower wages in other countries made UK industry uneconomic.
4. They are not tied to raw materials.
5. Transport and labour

Page 73 Industry in LEDCs
1. Newly industrialising Country
2. To protect their own industries from competition.
3. Nike or Union Carbide Corporation.
4. Cheap labour means bigger profits.
5. 12 000 dead, 500 000 injured

Managing Resources
Quick Test Answers
Page 75 Tourism
1. A visit that involves an overnight stay.
2. Longer holidays, higher wages
3. Climate, scenery, ecology, culture, activities.
4. Employment and increased protection of the environment.
5. Areas that attract the most visitors.

Page 77 Tourism
1. Seaside holidays.
2. Package holidays.
3. Tourism provides jobs and money.
4. Sunny, average temperature 25°C, low rainfall.
5. Encouraging smaller groups of high spending tourists, while protecting the environment.

Page 79 Resources
1. Any part of the environment used by people to live.
2. Population growth and world development.
3. Replacing one resource with another.
4. Agreement to achieve sustainable development at a local level.
5. Landfill sites

Page 81 Energy and environment

1. More efficient cars and appliances.
2. Population growth and economic development.
3. Upland or offshore areas with strong, reliable winds.
4. The trapping of solar energy in the Earth's atmosphere.
5. Human combustion of fossil fuels, deforestation and methane production.

Development
Quick Test Answers
Page 83 Development

1. Increase in income and wealth.
2. Northern hemisphere
3. Human Development Index combines economic and social development indicators.
4. People who get sick from dirty water are unable to work.
5. Small-scale, low-tech and involves local people.

Page 85 Trade and aid

1. The exchange of goods and services between countries.
2. The difference between value of imports and exports.
3. LEDCs export raw materials, MEDCs export manufactured goods.
4. Trade that ensures the producers in LEDCs are paid a fair price.
5. Aid money must be spent on goods or services from the donor country.

Answers to practice questions
Page 86 Population

1. Demographic transition model (1)
2. Birth rates remain high (1), death rates fall (1), population grows rapidly (1)
3. Death rates are low (1), birth rates are even lower (1), population is falling (1).
4. For example; Australia (1), North Africa (1)
5. Steep relief (1), extreme climate (1), dense vegetation such as rainforest (1), soils which are not fertile.
6. Percentage of males and females (1), percentage of different age groups (1), life expectancy (1), birth rate (1), death rate (1), infant mortality rate (1)
7. MEDC = narrowing base (1), vertical sides (1), wide peak (1), LEDC = wide base (1), steep sides (1), narrow peak (1)
8. Causes = war (1), quality of life (1), work (1), family (1), effects = Urbanisation (1), urban problems (1), problems in the countryside (1), resentment and racism (1), benefits to migrants (1), benefits to host country (1)

Page 87 Settlement

1. Increase in the percentage of people living in cities. (1)
2. A = Central Business District (1), B = shanty towns (1), C = medium-cost housing (1)
3. Low-quality housing in LEDCs (1), built by migrants from waste materials (1), may later be improved by using permanent building materials. (1)
4. Named example (1), self-help schemes (1), are when residents are sold cheap building materials by the government (1), site and service schemes (1), are when people are provided with plots of land (1), with basic services such as water and electricity (1), and are allowed to build their own homes. (1)
5. In MEDCs high quality housing is found on the outskirts (1), in LEDCs high quality housing is found in the inner city (1), MEDC settlements do not have squatter settlements. (1)
6. A CBD contains shops (1), offices (1), buildings are high rise (1)
7. Problems include unemployment (1), crime (1), transport problems (1), lack of services (1), deteriorating housing (1), falling house prices (1)
8. Named example (1), improvements include urban regeneration (1), wasteland re-developed with offices, shops and leisure facilities (1), urban redevelopment (1), poor quality housing replaced with new (1), gentrification (1), poor quality housing upgraded (1), integrated transport systems (1), new ring roads, and light railways. (1)

Page 88 Agriculture

1. A = mixed farming (1), B = arable (1), C = sheep and beef farming (1)
2. A combination of arable and pastoral farming. (1)
3. Rainfall (1), temperature (1), growing season (1), altitude (1), relief (1), soil (1)
4. Labour (1), market (1), accessibility (1), subsidies (1), quotas (1), attitudes (1)
5. Flatter land (1), fertile, well-drained soils (1), high-quality grass (1), mild winters (1), reliable rainfall (1), rapid access to large urban markets (1).
6. Common Agricultural Policy (1), provides grants and subsidies (1), for farmers in difficult areas (1), and price support (1), for certain crops (1)
7. Produces food for the farmers family (1)
8. Introduction of capital intensive farming methods in LEDCs. (1)
9. High Yield Variety crops (1), faster growing (1), give increased yield (1), fertilisers (1), used to feed crops (1), herbicides (1), control weeds (1), pesticides (1), control insects (1), irrigation used to water crops (1), machinery introduced (1)
10. HYV crops are expensive (1), and need expensive pesticides (1), and fertilisers (1), mechanisation increased rural unemployment (1), monoculture increases risk from disease (1), products are exported, poor cannot afford them (1)

Page 89 Industry

1. Extraction or production of raw materials. (1)
2. Primary products are processed or manufactured into secondary goods (1), secondary goods are sold by tertiary industry, shops. (1)
3. A = NIC (1), B = LEDC (1), C = MEDC (1)
4. Development of new industries (1), such as manufacturing or tourism (1)
5. Named example (1), industries with heavy raw materials locate close to them (1), because of the transport costs (1), technical jobs require a skilled workforce (1), assembly jobs require a cheap workforce (1), location of market (1), concentrated or dispersed market. (1)
6. Very large companies with offices and factories all over the world. (1)
7. Low tax rates (1), minimise bureaucracy – red tape (1), relax planning laws (1), relax health and safety laws (1), relax environmental laws (1), devalue their currency to make labour cheaper (1), provide a well educated workforce (1)
8. Named example (1), Advantages = provides jobs (1), increases wealth (1), taxes are paid to government (1), people learn skills (1), infrastructure and services may be improved (1), Disadvantages = TNCs are powerful and may influence government decisions (1), Profits are transferred to headquarters in MEDCs (1), jobs may be low skill (1), and dangerous (1), wages are low (1), may cause damage to the environment (1)

Page 90 Managing resources

1. Oil (1)
2. Nuclear (1)
3. Increased (1), by 3000 million tonnes oil equivalent (1), increase has been uneven (1)
4. Population growth (1), more people will need more energy (1), development (1), as people become richer they demand more energy (1)
5. Increase energy supply (1), by increased electricity production (1), using alternative energy such as solar (1), reduce demand (1), by recycling (1) persuading people to save energy (1)
6. Climate (1), scenery (1), ecology (1), culture (1), activities (1)
7. Employment (1), economic benefit to the area (1), money may be invested in infrastructure, health or education (1)
8. Eco-tourism/green tourism (1), mass tourism is discouraged (1), small groups of wealthy tourists are encouraged (1), tourists stay with local people (1), rather than building new hotels (1), new hotels must be built below tree height (1), tourists educated about local culture and customs (1), tourist tax is used to protect, conserve and repair environment. (1)

Page 91 Development

1. The total value of all goods and services produced by a country in one year, divided by the population to give an average per person. (1)
2. Cost of living varies between different countries (1), development is about quality of life, not just money. (1)
3. Birth rate (1), death rate (1), life expectancy (1), infant mortality (1), population per doctor (1), literacy (1), years in education (1), Human Development Index (1)
4. Contaminated water causes illness and disease (1), such as cholera, dysentery and diarrhoea (1), sick people are unable to work (1), this places a strain on healthcare services (1), also hours are wasted collecting water from long distances. (1)
5. 0.7% of GNP (1)
6. Norway (1), Sweden (1), Finland (1)
7. Emergency aid (1), short term disaster relief (1), long term aid (1), e.g. education or training (1), multilateral aid (1), arranged by international organisations such as banks (1), bilateral aid (1), arranged by individual governments (1), tied aid (1), money must be spent on goods from donor country (1), NGO aid (1), aid from charities. (1)
8. Aid may be a loan and cause more debt (1), food aid may causes prices to fall (1), and put farmers out of business (1), aid might include inappropriate high technology items (1), the rich may benefit most (1), aid money may be stolen by corrupt officials. (1)
9. MEDCs export mainly manufactured goods (1), which are high value (1), LEDCs export mainly primary goods (1), which are low value (1), the price of manufactured goods is increasing faster than the price of primary goods. (1)